WHAT THE PRAYERS
OF JESUS TELL US
ABOUT THE HEART
OF GOD

WHAT *the* PRAYERS *of* JESUS TELL US ABOUT *the* HEART *of* GOD

SHANE STANFORD

ABINGDON PRESS
NASHVILLE

WHAT THE PRAYERS OF JESUS
TELL US ABOUT THE HEART OF GOD

Copyright © 2015 by Shane Stanford

Library of Congress Cataloging-in-Publication Data

Stanford, Shane, 1970-
  What the prayers of Jesus tell us about the heart of God / Shane Stanford.
    pages cm
  Includes bibliographical references.
  ISBN 978-1-4267-7425-6 (binding: soft back) 1. Jesus Christ—Prayers. 2. God—Love. I. Title.
  BV229.S73 2015
  232.9'54—dc23

                                                    2015005947

15 16 17 18 19 20 21 22 23 24—10 9 8 7 6 5 4 3 2 1
MANUFACTURED IN THE UNITED STATES OF AMERICA

For Pokey,
whose love and care transcend "more than words."

For my girls, Sarai Grace, Juli Anna, and Emma Leigh,
whose spiritual journeys inspire me more and more every day. You
are definitely "how you pray," and your prayers
are beautiful.

Contents

Contents

INTRODUCTION

If you have spent any amount of time reading the Gospels, you may have noticed that Jesus prayed and spent quiet time with God on a regular basis. Prayer was an important part of Jesus' routine, and it was especially critical to his relationship with God. There are more than sixty occasions in the Gospels when Jesus goes away to "pray," "meditate," "be alone," and so on. These appear at various times in Jesus' ministry, and they cross different thresholds as far as importance and focus are concerned. But these are not ritualistic prayers, offered in service as a rabbi or teacher. Prayer for Jesus in this context is private conversation with God the Father. These are not simply interludes for some extended Eastern meditative experience. Instead, they are part heartbeat, part instruction, part love letter, and part plea from Jesus to the Father. These prayers are not just about communication; they are also the first time in the history of the universe that the persons of God spoke across actual time and space with each other. The natural "dance" or *perichoresis* that existed in the trinitarian relationship before the

1

Incarnation found a new way to connect the divinity of the *Logos*, the Word of God, with the humanity of Jesus of Nazareth. Therefore, we as believers should not miss that this form of prayer—no longer just our pleas or persuasion—was created as an incarnated means of sharing between the heart of God and the heart of God's creation. If that didn't just send goose bumps up your arms, then just hang on for what comes later.

When we break down the sixty-some-odd prayers that Jesus prayed (or times that he taught on prayer) in Scripture, we discover that Jesus' prayers fall into five major focus areas:

> Prayer Focus 1: Jesus Prays for Our Relationship with the Father
>
> Prayer Focus 2: Jesus Prays for God's Wisdom and Guidance in Us
>
> Prayer Focus 3: Jesus Prays for Our Unity
>
> Prayer Focus 4: Jesus Prays for Lives that Bring Glory to God
>
> Prayer Focus 5: Jesus Prays for Our Consistency in Prayer

These five focus areas represent the key intersections of much of Jesus' ministry, both as a conduit for how the Father is working through him and as a catalyst for what he intends and hopes for the disciples to become. Jesus' prayers are the expression of the core of his "prayer life"—a broader experience that goes way beyond the actual moment of prayer.

But understanding the specific prayers of Jesus requires more than simply working through these five focus areas. In fact, to comprehend the importance of Jesus' prayer life, we have to be willing to personally invest and respond within the context of three parts of Jesus' life and ministry. These parts are:

- Jesus' personal relationship with the Father;
- Jesus' confidence in himself and in his earthly ministry; and
- Jesus' hopes and confidence in his disciples' ministry.

These three areas of Jesus' earthly life become the essence for understanding Jesus' incarnation as being "fully God" and "fully human," with the divine nature wrapped within the nature of his humanity. The one place where this essence shows itself most clearly is in the prayer life of Jesus. We may see glimpses of the intersection of these three areas of Jesus' person in his miracles, in his teachings, in his human interactions—but nowhere do we meet the person of Jesus more completely than in the words, routine, and intentions of his prayers and his prayer life. Of all that you read, this should be the easiest to comprehend—for I would argue that our own clearest expressions of our spiritual journey are experienced within our prayers and our devotional time.

Now, just to be clear—Jesus was fully God. He dwelt with the Trinity, meaning Jesus was part of the divine relationship of God the Father, God the Son, and God the Holy Spirit. Jesus of Nazareth was the physical incarnation of the second person of the Trinity come to earth. God the Father and God the Holy Spirit enveloped the incarnated Christ through their personal presence with him in Creation. The Holy Spirit interacted with Jesus through healings, miracles, and the supernatural experience of God's power. But God the Father interacted primarily through these "set-aside" moments of prayer and solitude with the Son. Jesus' personal knowledge of the Father is beyond compare. But their interactions before the Incarnation knew no bounds of time or space. To know that God would make himself subject to living in the form of flesh and to the limitations of what the Incarnation would mean for God literally takes my breath away. Truly, the sacrifice that was the Incarnation, displayed in the obedience of the Son, Jesus Christ (see Philippians 2), began with and included the Father's sacrifice of God the Father's interaction with the Son. Thus, the entire experience of the Incarnation—and not just the Crucifixion and Resurrection—evoked the notion of God's great sacrifice. Prayer was the bridge for addressing the chasm of flesh and time between the persons of the Trinity.

Imagine being so close to someone that you experienced

*A*nd it came to pass, that, as he was praying in a certain place, when he ceased, one of his disciples said unto him, Lord, teach us to pray, as John also taught his disciples.

And he said unto them, When ye pray, say, Our Father which art in heaven, Hallowed be thy name. Thy kingdom come. Thy will be done, as in heaven, so in earth.

Give us day by day our daily bread.

And forgive us our sins; for we also forgive every one that is indebted to us. And lead us not into temptation; but deliver us from evil.

Luke 11:1-4 (KJV)

each other's next breath. You thought the same thoughts and rejoiced with the same joys. You watched the same brokenness unfold and even developed the same plan for the other's future. But in order for your next steps to work, one of you would have to "limit" yourself, including the way in which you could relate to the other.

That is what happened between the Father and the Son. At the moment of Jesus' birth in Bethlehem, the members of the Trinity literally set themselves apart from one another within certain bounds, not in how they felt about one another or in their intentions for one another, but in the nature and nuance of what it meant to "be." Therefore, whereas before the Incarnation the next expression of God the Father or God the Son to each other could be shared (as Scripture hints) as simply as the Spirit moving like the wind, after the Incarnation, prayer became their element of communication and intimacy.

And yet, it does not stop there. The nature of prayer changed for humanity too. The Holy Spirit became not just a messenger but a conduit for the prayers of Jesus—and for our prayers as well. Thus, through the incarnation of Jesus, it became possible for us to tap into the "God net," if you will, so that we, after Pentecost, might connect directly to the heart of God—a divine being no longer waiting on the mountain or even walking beside us on the shores of the lake, but living within us, navigating our prayers, even speaking for us when the words did not come (Romans 8:26).

Therefore, the prayers of Jesus became both the vehicle for Jesus' own communication with the Father and the framework for our new means of communication with God as well. That is why Jesus' prayers (as markers for understanding the deeper nature of Jesus' prayer life) are important on several levels.

The prayers of Jesus detail the relationship between the Father and the Son during Jesus' earthly ministry. This example is crucial to understanding the plan of salvation as expressed through God's sending of God's Son, but also the practical nature of God's love and affinity for creation and God's people. Jesus' prayers lead us through "doorways" below the surface level of Jesus' relationships.

The prayers of Jesus offer a framework for how we should live our own lives in relationship to God. They are not just about Jesus' relationship to God; they also serve as an open door through which he believes each of us should draw close to the Father. Proximity of our lives to the life of God becomes the central conversation in many of Jesus' prayers.

The prayers of Jesus also provide an example of how and who we are in relationship with one another. Jesus spends much time using his prayers to describe his relationship and interactions with the Father. But although that is the primary dynamic—how we too should relate to the Father—we also see an example in the relationship of Father and Son of how we should relate to one another in love, grace, and communion.

Therefore, I do not believe it is too bold to say that Jesus' prayer life stands at the center of how Jesus' divine relationship with the Father and his human relationships with his followers should (and did) exist and function. Again, there is no mechanism in Scripture that serves as the pathway in Scripture for the personal, intimate interaction leading from God to Jesus to us and then back to God, more than the prayer life of Jesus.

Jesus' prayer life, which he tells us in Matthew 6 is the model or frame for our own prayer lives, becomes the first and primary link by which we connect with God and then with God's people. As a theologian friend loved to advise me, "Prayer is the heavenly conversation translated for earthly experience." Wow!

Throughout this book, we will see how the rhythm of Jesus' communication with the Father defines and demonstrates the power and importance of the prayer life of Jesus. As you experience this, I pray that, like me, you won't read the passages about Jesus going away to be with the Father in quite the same way ever again. We will also be exploring the five prayer focus areas in which Jesus' prayers set powerful examples for each of us to follow. Next, we will see how the prayers of Jesus frame the broader relationships of Jesus' prayer life within his earthly ministry and journey. And finally, we will unveil how the prayer focus areas affect how we pray for our own needs, for one another, and for the world.

In writing this book and inviting us to take this journey together, I have three goals. First, after you read this book, I want you to be able to view the complete, daily life of Jesus in a different way than you did before. There is so much for us to learn about how his life and daily routines look so very much like our own, except that Jesus seems much less surprised or caught off guard than we do by how life unfolds.

Second, I pray that you will take note of the prayer focus areas as more than just suggestions from Jesus, but rather as critical links to how we not only come to know Jesus better, but also how we come to know one another better.

And finally, when you've finished reading and we've come to the end of this part of our journey together, I hope you will walk back into Jesus' life and get to know him even better. He is truly special, genuine, and the dearest friend a person could have.

So sit back, grab your Bible, and get ready to take some time to "go away with Jesus." You won't be disappointed.

At that time Jesus said, "I praise you, Father, Lord of heaven and earth, because you've hidden these things from the wise and intelligent and have shown them to babies. Indeed, Father, this brings you happiness.

"My Father has handed all things over to me. No one knows the Son except the Father. And nobody knows the Father except the Son and anyone to whom the Son wants to reveal him.

"Come to me, all you who are struggling hard and carrying heavy loads, and I will give you rest. Put on my yoke, and learn from me. I'm gentle and humble. And you will find rest for yourselves. My yoke is easy to bear, and my burden is light."

Matthew 11:25-30

JESUS PRAYS FOR OUR RELATIONSHIP WITH THE FATHER

Matthew 11:25-30

In Matthew 11:25, we experience one of the prayers of Jesus set within Scripture detailing Jesus' remarks about those who are struggling hard and carrying heavy loads. However, we may not realize that this section follows a prayer of Jesus in which he asks the Father for his disciples to experience a relationship with the Father as he himself is in relationship with the Father. It is easy to strip the latter part from the passage and focus on it alone. It is emotional and powerful. However, to separate the notion of Jesus welcoming those who are tired and weary apart from the former prayer to the Father about Jesus' own relationship with God and his prayer that the disciples will experience exactly the same context does injustice to the full meaning of the Scripture. Here are the two passages together:

At that time Jesus said, "I praise you, Father, Lord of heaven and earth, because you've hidden these things from the wise and intelligent and have shown them to babies. Indeed, Father, this brings you happiness.

"My Father has handed all things over to me. No one knows the Son except the Father. And nobody knows the Father except the Son and anyone to whom the Son wants to reveal him.

"Come to me, all you who are struggling hard and carrying heavy loads, and I will give you rest. Put on my yoke, and learn from me. I'm gentle and humble. And you will find rest for yourselves. My yoke is easy to bear, and my burden is light." (Matthew 11:25-30)

I have heard for many years in ministry that our culture wants something that truly matters; thus we don't care as much about the normal church conversations. For instance, there's a recent study that says approximately 75 percent of all Christians today are not worried about what particular denomination of church they attend. This study also revealed that most people are not worried about church location, size, or facility options. Instead, most Christians prefer to worship within a congregation that fits deeply with how they view what it means to live out their beliefs in the world.[1] Stated more clearly, most believers want to belong to a worship community that truly embodies what they proclaim in Jesus Christ. In essence, they want a relationship with God and others that evokes a deeper response from their souls.

My own standards changed several years ago after a serious medical illness. I realized, like so many of my brothers and sisters in the ministry, that I could spend my entire career in service to the institution of Christianity without making much difference for "following Christ." I could give my life to an organization where I made more money or received greater perks for hours of preparation and hard work. Certainly, I didn't enter into ministry without much prayer or meditation. But the church, like any institution, creates responsibilities that fill up our lives with "urgent" matters instead of focusing us on the truly *important*. That is not what my vocation or any commitment to the church should mean. I went into ministry to give my life to something more. From the very beginning of my ministry journey, I have believed the *church* is the hope of the world—not the denomination or the organization, but the body of men and women committed to one primary point of reference, namely, Jesus.

We learn in the prayers of Jesus that we should want something more than nameplates and accolades. Whether we fully realize it or not, Jesus understood that we seek a relationship with the Father that transforms our life. We don't have to become something more than we are—no, we need only take hold of that which is already being offered to us through relationship with the Father. Jesus says in John 14, essentially, "the more you know me, the more you're able to experience the power of what the Father wants to do in you." Do you want that? I can't imagine that we would want anything less from our experience with Christ. You and I should want more than religion; we should want a deep, abiding relationship that changes us personally and then sends us to change the world.

I've been in service to my faith and religion my whole adult life, and I have learned, sometimes the hard way, that there is so much more to one than to the other. There's more than simply belonging to a church, volunteering for a ministry, serving on a committee, or even sharing your resources. Jesus says real faith is first about relationship with the Father. In fact, Jesus believes so deeply about this relationship that he makes it a major focus of his time away with the Father and his teaching of the disciples.

However, it is important to realize that Jesus' request is set within the framework of his own relationship with the Father. For God, the Incarnation (Jesus becoming fully human as well as fully divine) was not just a vessel for Jesus to walk among humanity. It was the means for Jesus to speak within and for our humanity. Instead of God being seen as a distant figure set on a mountaintop, handing down proclamations to his followers, God became a living, breathing part of creation so as to both experience and encourage a new connection between God and humanity. And one of Jesus' first requests of the Father is that the same relationship that God the Father and the Son shared would be available for humanity's relationship with God as well.

What does a relationship with the Father look like? According to Jesus' own teachings, four principles define it.

Relationship with the Father Is Intentional

The power of intentionality imparts an air of authenticity to a relationship. There's nothing that says more to a person in a relationship than for you to do something intentional for or with that person. This past Mother's Day, I was so proud of my children. They were so intentional about celebrating with their mom and telling her how important she is to them. One card they gave her read, "We love you, and we so appreciate everything you do for us." Each of them signed it and offered a more personal word. It was heartfelt.

Now, most of us have been there: You get close to Mother's Day and forget the special day is coming up so quickly. You buy a card, a gift, and give it to Mom at dinner, but that's not the same as being so intentional as to convey a personal message telling her how much you appreciate her. Of course, you don't have to buy any gifts or make cards in order for your mother to know that you love and appreciate her. And you certainly shouldn't wait until Mother's Day to offer your thoughts and thanks to her. It is the intentionality that makes the difference.

That's the same principle that should guide our relationship with the Father. God has gone to deliberate lengths by giving his own Son. There was nothing more intentional the Father could give for you and me. His gift was personal—yet, even those words don't fully express what that gift meant. When was the last time you spent fifteen minutes uninterrupted in relationship with God? You want to know why that's sometimes so hard for us? It's not just some spiritual attention-deficit issue. I believe that the adversary is so scared of us spending intentional, quality time with the Father because he knows that when we spend such time with God, it changes us and causes us to become change agents for everyone we meet in the world. Intentionality in our relationship with God is critical.

Look at what Paul says in Romans 1:16. This comes at the end of a passage where Paul is being challenged as to what he believes in this world. He says, "I'm not ashamed of the gospel." Paul wants to be intentional about what he believes when his faith is being called into question. And he says, "It is God's own power for salvation to all who have faith in God."

16

Our relationship with God must be a conscious choice. It must occupy a particular part of our lives if for no other reason than God made you a specific priority in his life through Jesus.

Last fall I toured some of the retirement homes where members of my church live. One day one of our members said to me, "I want you to meet Jack." So, I went to meet Jack in his beautiful-but-modest apartment. He was an older gentleman who had been in the retirement home for several years. Jack is English, and he invited me to have tea with him one afternoon.

We met the next week as well, and I enjoyed the tea and conversation very much. As I sat with him, I saw a large box over in the corner of his tiny apartment. It was a new television. Jack is on a modest income and had told the deliverymen that he did not need anyone to set up the television. However, Jack did not know where to start, and the television had remained basically unopened. I really don't know what I was thinking, but I volunteered to help. "Jack," I said, "I'll come back and set up your television for you."

Now, I actually am not bad with such tasks—I just don't have any time to do them. But I had made the promise, and I had no intention of letting Jack down. So, on another day that week, I spent the afternoon setting up Jack's new 48-inch HDTV. It was beautiful.

However, Jack called my office a few days later and said,

"Pastor Shane, something terrible has happened." I thought maybe Jack was sick or in the hospital. But he said, "My television is acting up something awful!" Later that evening, a friend and I went to Jack's apartment. Jack was right—his TV was not the way we had originally set it up according to the instructions. We looked at the television from every angle, working from the beginning to the end of the instructions and the guidebook.

After a little more than an hour, we found the problem: Somewhere along the way, Jack had hit one single button that reset the TV back to its manufacturer's settings. So now, none of what we had taught him about how to operate the television worked or made sense. So we fixed the settings, instructed Jack never to touch that particular button again, and left. I remember leaving his condominium village that day and telling the guy next to me, "You know what? I live my life a lot like the way Jack's television is acting. God makes these new adjustments in my life. Everything is brighter and clearer. But then, life gets too comfortable or too uncomfortable. I get restless, careless, or just selfish. That is when I restore the factory settings and go back to the old way of living. How much time have I wasted in this world by simply living by the old defaults, instead of deciding to be intentional and better in my relationship with Jesus?"

Are you living by the old defaults today instead of trusting the intentional ways God has worked to change your life? Maybe you go to church. You go to Sunday school. You read your Bible every once in a while. You might even throw an occasional devotional in there. But God has so much more for you, and he is intentional about you taking hold of it.

I remember a wonderful friend of mine who said, "Shane, Jesus' death for us is as extravagant a gift as we ever could be given; why would we want to give him back something in return that doesn't matter at all to us?" Our relationships with the Father must be intentional.

Our Relationship with the Father Is Intimate

Several months ago I preached a sermon series on the biblical definition of *intimacy*. One key element of defining biblical intimacy is to distinguish it as covenantal instead of contractual in nature. When you're in a contract with someone, you don't need intimacy. And for many of us, we enter into our relationship with God as though we are in a contract with God: *God, if you do* this, *I'll do* this. *If you show up* here, *I'll show up at church. If you'll make me financially stable, then I'll give my money back to you.* It goes on and on. We have all these conditions for how and when we will be in relationship with God. Sure, we may never discuss it this way, but this is how many of us live out our relationship with God. It is often easier to live our most important relationships in a contractual manner—where all the responsibilities and actions are clearly defined and expected. But contractual lives are not *intimate* lives.

Jesus prayed that we might know the Father intimately as he knew the Father. Now, think about that. You and I are supposed to know the Father the way Jesus knows the Father, and has there ever been a relationship more intimate than the one that exists between the Father and the Son of the Trinity? We are supposed to be so close to God that it's like taking our next breath. The early Christian theologians strove to explain the nature of the Trinity using such words as *perichoresis*, which is a classic theological description of the intimacy of the persons of God interacting together—much like two people involved in a close, personal dance. Their point was that the relationship within the Trinity was so intimate it was as if they were existing in an alive space or moment, such as dancing an intimate dance together—moving in complete and perfect rhythm and order.[2] Doesn't that sound comforting to have that kind of relationship with God? And yet many of us stay locked in contractual relationships where our closeness is measured by what we can offer to one another. The problem is that our love can cross only as far as we can reach and understand it. In both cases, our fragile humanity is very limited and offers little to us during the more difficult moments of life.

The Bible is clear that we are created to live in covenantal relationships. I once told a bride and groom, "You can live your marriage as friends, being very familiar with each other, but that's not the same as being intimate with each other. I've known many women, but I've only been intimate with one, and that's my wife. And there's an incredible difference." Everyone in the bridal party, as well as some in the congregation, got the message. Many started to chuckle. But everyone who heard me knew *exactly* what I was saying.

God says, "I want an intimate relationship with you." Acts 4:10-12 tells us,

> Jesus Christ the Nazarene—whom you crucified but whom God raised from the dead…is the stone you builders re jected; he has become the cornerstone! Salvation can be found in no one else. Throughout the whole world, no other name has been given among humans through which we must be saved.

How intimate is your relationship with God supposed to be? It is at the center of not only when we take the next breath but also *why* we take the next breath at all.

Now, please hear me—I have experienced this depth of intimate relationship at this level with God only a few times in my life. Why? Because I am a broken, fragile, sinful person.

But every day I awake with this as my goal. No one is going to be perfect in his or her daily walk with God, but it is well worth the effort! Since my open heart surgery nearly ten years ago, I tell my wife I may not be the perfect husband, but I certainly want to try. Jesus says, "I have given you my most-special intimate gift—my life as a sacrifice—and it is by that gift that the world is saved." Jesus did that because he loves us, not because he was under contract to do so.

Our relationships have to be intimate.

Our Relationship with the Father Is Instructional

Over the last two years, God has provided four mentors in my life who have become wonderful, strong guides for my spiritual journey. Several years ago, I realized how many people God had placed along my journey to show me a better way and to encourage me along the path. I believe there are two parts to every one of our relationships: (1) a teacher and (2) a student.

First, I believe God provides us with a mentor whom God puts into our lives to provide guidance and encouragement. However, I believe that God also provides someone for *us* to mentor—a student to teach and guide as well. This is not just my perception—the Bible is filled with one example after another: Moses and Joshua, Peter and Mark, Barnabas and Paul, Paul and Timothy.

At that very moment, Jesus overflowed with joy from the Holy Spirit and said, "I praise you, Father, Lord of heaven and earth, because you've hidden these things from the wise and intelligent and shown them to babies. Indeed, Father, this brings you happiness. My Father has handed all things over to me. No one knows who the Son is except the Father, or who the Father is except the Son and anyone to whom the Son wants to reveal him."

Luke 10:21-22

Every relationship born in Jesus is instructional. Look at what it says in 1 Thessalonians 5:9-11: "God didn't intend for us to suffer his wrath but rather to possess salvation through our Lord Jesus Christ. Jesus died for us so that, whether we are awake or asleep, we will live together with him. So continue encouraging each other and building each other up, just like you are doing already."

Let me ask you something: Are you being shaped by a mentor who has been down this same road? You're never too old to be taught and shaped. But have you also taken responsibility to help shape others?

As I mentioned before, even after twenty-five years in ministry, God has provided four new individuals at this stage of my journey to guide, shape, and encourage me. One of those four is Maxie Dunnam. Although Maxie is nearly eighty years old, he has found a new season of great hope and significance in his ministry. He is like a spiritual father in my life. When I talk with him or go to lunch with him, he inspires me with his drive (and scares me to death with his driving!).

Maxie and I don't agree on every issue. We come from different generations and angles in so many discussions. But I watch him, and his life is a testament teaching me about God's provisions and hope for me. What keeps him going is that he gets a chance to teach others what God has taught him. Yet even in his life, at this part of his journey, he's still seeking after those who can teach him. I watch it every day. Maxie gets excited when we talk with someone who can share a new word from God. It is as if he is just starting in ministry himself. I hope I never forget the power of what it means that Jesus died to transform our lives and our relationships. Thanks, Maxie.

When I was a sophomore in college, God put a woman named Polly Macintosh into my life. She was a frail widow who loved the Lord dearly. Throughout my college years and into my ministry as a student pastor, Miss Polly and I met weekly to talk and just share our love of God. I went to seminary under the care of her authentic prayers. And when the first church following my seminary training wouldn't take me as their pastor because of my health, Miss Polly donated the money for my salary to be the associate pastor at her church. She literally saved my ministry. I served her local church for two years. I was then appointed to start a new congregation.

I remember being in her home, having lunch with her just before setting out to plant a new church. She said, "I want to give you a gift." And I said, "You've paid for my salary for two years—I don't need a gift." And she said, "No, I want to give you something that matters." And I thought, *Trust me: money matters!* Miss Polly had a lot of resources, but it didn't matter to her unless she could use them for something significant.

She left for a moment and then came back with a beautifully wrapped small gift box. In it was her husband's treasured Bible. Her late husband was the light of her life, and he had loved the Lord almost as much as Miss Polly did. They did not have any children, and so their relationship had been at the center of their lives. They taught so many others about marriage and hope through their example. I knew this was one of the most important gifts she could give me. In this Bible were Pete's markings and sermon notes. He had written down important passages and verses to remember. I knew how much it meant for Miss Polly to hand this over to me. I didn't have the honor of knowing Pete personally, but his Bible is sitting on my shelf now, and it's a reminder to me of the ways God continues to teach us through the faithful testimonies of others. Pete invested heavily in others and is still changing our world.

Our relationships are to be intentional. They are to be intimate. And they are to be instructional.

Our Relationship with the Father Is Intercessory

Intercession is the process of "re-placing" oneself within the journey of someone else as a means of support, protection, or guidance. Intercession is at the center of God's relationship for us in Christ. Through the Incarnation, God literally stepped into our journey through his Son, Jesus Christ. But according to Jesus, to draw close to God also means to draw close to one another, and we too take on intercession as part of our relationships.

This should not sound so foreign. Most of our covenantal relationships at some point or another require us to stand in the gap for someone else—maybe even for someone whom we do not know. Or as Jesus mentioned, we may be called to intercede for someone who would not intercede for us (see Matthew 5:44; Luke 6:28). Of course, reading back on the story of Jesus the Christ and the cross, we realize that Jesus did just that for all of us, even for those of us who don't understand what he did or who would even refuse it if we did understand it. To follow Jesus, and to experience the fullness of relationship with God, calls for a deeper connection to God. Thus, our relationships must mirror the relationship between Jesus and the Father. And in praying for us to experience that relationship, Jesus also prays for us to allow that relationship to move us to do the unthinkable, the uncomfortable...even the unreasonable. Who would put their lives on the line for those who don't love them back? Jesus did.

Are you willing to stand in the gap for someone you don't know or someone who doesn't appreciate what you do for him or her? I believe one of the most profound passages in Scripture is when Jesus says, in effect, "Don't talk about building a relationship only with people you love, because even those who don't believe in God will do that. But will you invest or intersect your life even for someone who hates you? Because that's the real nature of what a relationship with God means in this world" (Matthew 5:43-47, paraphrased). You want to change the world? Show that you love the world the way Jesus loves you.

Recently, I tweeted out the statistic that 75 to 90 percent of people who will come to know the Lord this year will do so through a friend or a family member.[3] I wish it was preaching that drew most people into relationship with Christ. That would certainly make for more job security for me! However, the truth speaks overwhelmingly to something else: It's *you*! Believers; Christians; people sitting in the pews are the greatest evangelists the church has. Your relationships with family and friends are the church's great evangelism fields. Are you ready to go?

Jesus prayed for this moment, this day right now, when, in the Great Commission, he said, "Go into the world and make disciples…baptizing them, and teaching them to obey everything that I have taught you" (Matthew 28:19-20, paraphrased). These words have become so familiar that we often miss the importance of each phrase. For example, first, "Go into the world" is written in the present imperative tense, suggesting that we make disciples "as we go" about our daily business. Where does the majority of our daily business happen? Yes, with friends and family.

Second, many could read "baptizing them" as meaning only a liturgical format where we see clergy officiating. But to a first-century Jew, baptism was the rite of inclusion into their culture and faith. Who do we include in our journey? Our family and friends.

Third, most of our opportunities for "teaching them" happen not with strangers but with those to whom we are closest. Who are those people in our lives? Once again, they are friends and family. The Great Commission is a personal invitation to connect to the most "personal people" in our lives. To draw close in our relationship with the Father means learning to intercede as Christ would do for us.

The Dangling Cord

Years ago, Father John Powell told the story of Norma Jean Mortenson in an article that appeared in the 1990 issue of *Dynamic Preaching*. Norma Jean—whom we know today as film star Marilyn Monroe—overdosed on sleeping pills in 1962 at the age of thirty-six.

According to Father Powell's article, in the last moments of her life, Marilyn called an actor friend and told him she had taken the pills, intending to take her own life. He allegedly replied, à la Rhett Butler, "Frankly, my dear, I don't give a damn."

As Marilyn died, the article states, she dropped the phone, leaving it dangling from its cord to be discovered by her maid the next morning.

There are so many stories, rumors, and urban legends surrounding the life and death of Marilyn Monroe, and Father Powell's piece contained both highly substantiated and controversial elements of her life and final days. The real truth may never be known. But one thing seems certain: this loving girl named Norma Jean, abandoned by a sick mom, bounced around life, abused and alone, until she took on a new identity in search of meaning. Sadly, even then, the beautiful Marilyn Monroe lived a glamorous life void of the very things she needed and craved to be truly alive. The debate over whether someone quoting Rhett Butler hung up on her in those last moments does not negate the fact that for much of her life she believed no one was on the "other end of the line" who really cared.

Jesus knew we could go only so far in this world on our own. Sure, we can be smart, spiritual, faithful, and "good." But we can never be smart enough, spiritual enough, faithful enough, or good enough. And so, one of Jesus' deepest prayers, when he went away to be alone with the Father, was for you and me to have the same relationship that he had with the Father. He knew that the closer we were to our Father, the less the world would work itself into our vulnerable areas, and distract and disrupt our journey. Jesus wanted us to know that there is always someone on the other end of the line who cares more than words can express.

God wants a deep, personal, covenantal relationship with you, and he will do anything to make that happen. In fact, he did: God gave us Jesus.

I will ask the Father, and he will send another Companion, who will be with you forever. This Companion is the Spirit of Truth, whom the world can't receive because it neither sees him nor recognizes him. You know him, because he lives with you and will be with you.

John 14:16-17

I have revealed your name to the people you gave me from this world. They were yours and you gave them to me, and they have kept your word. Now they know that everything you have given me comes from you.

John 17:6-7

Prayer Focus 2

JESUS PRAYS FOR GOD'S WISDOM AND GUIDANCE IN US

John 14:1-19

In the last chapter, we learned that one of Jesus' focal points is for each of us to have a deep relationship with the Father—particularly along the same lines as Jesus' own relationship with the Father. The power of that relationship means significant things for us going forward in both our relationship with God and our relationships with one another.

The second prayer focus of Jesus is that God's wisdom and strength, not the wisdom and standards of the world, will shape our lives. As a parent, I am very conscious about what the world wants to teach my children as well as what the world expects from my life and my family. You don't have to spend much time watching modern culture and social media to understand the adversary's concerted effort to distract our families. Our children in particular are very vulnerable to the distractions of the world. The goal of these distractions is to replace God's standards for our lives with the standards of a broken world. On several occasions, Jesus prayed, almost prophetically, that the disciples would be shaped and filled, not with the wisdom of the world but with the wisdom of God. Jesus says, in essence, in John 17, "Father, if they're going to learn how to move forward and make decisions in this world, they must learn that from our example." Clearly, through the heart of the Gospel of John, Jesus' hope for the disciples has been bathed in prayer. John 14 is a perfect example of how Jesus' intentions for the disciples affect his prayers and, then, how his prayers inform his intentions.

In John 14, Jesus instructs the disciples to shape their journey with God's wisdom and truth. In fact, he shares that as their journey deepens, he will "ask the Father" to send a "Companion" to guide them (v. 16). Jesus describes this prayer focus as more than just another theological lesson. Instead, this is an expression of the deep relationship between the Father and the Son. Jesus understands that the world expects little but takes much from us. And oftentimes, we are left empty, having believed the lie but found little to "hang our hats on." Sound familiar? Our journey can come to completion only as it is equal to the wisdom and truth that guide it. Therefore, in this life, good intentions and great skill are not enough. We must possess something more.

John 13 and 14 describes three encounters Jesus has with his disciples that ultimately define this powerful prayer focus of Jesus. First, when Peter declares that he will stand for Jesus even to his own death, Jesus tells Peter that he is not ready, but then goes on to offer him and the other disciples hope for the future (13:36–14:4). Second, Thomas, knowing Jesus is about to leave them, asks how they'll know the way forward. Jesus answers Thomas by saying, "I am the way, the truth, and the life. No one comes to the Father except through me" (v. 6). Finally, Philip presses Jesus on how they will know how to find and follow the Father. Jesus responds by saying, in effect, "Simple...if you have seen me, you have seen the Father. Keep your eyes on me!" (vv. 8-9).

For all of the conversation in these two chapters, established around the very personal, troubled hearts of those asking these questions, the heartbeat of Jesus' message centers around relationship with the Father and provides so much more than what the world can offer. In simpler terms, Jesus encourages the disciples to find real life, real wisdom, and real truth by staying close to the Father. And thus, as the disciples are consumed by their uncertainty and fear, Jesus promises to pray for them and their future by asking God to send them a divine Companion. A specific prayer does not appear in the text, but we know that prayer is both the overflow of Jesus' relationship with the

Father and his intentions for those who follow him. Much as we need not ask if a mother prays for her son who goes off to war, we needn't wonder if Jesus prays for us; we know it as much by the relationship as by the actual act.

It is important not to miss the fact that as Jesus is talking about wisdom and truth and what it means to find real direction in this world, the conversation is set within the context of trouble. The Bible is clear that God works faithfully, and sometimes "best," in the midst of our most broken and most trying seasons. Jesus believed there's no better time in our lives to seek after real wisdom and real truth than when we are facing pushback, difficulties, or sorrows.

A Deeper Look at John 14

In John 14, Jesus' disciples know that something's up. Jesus has talked several times now about uncertainties coming in the future, making it clear that there are troubles around the corner. Jesus sees on their faces that they are unsettled and uncomfortable. The disciples are looking for direction. But that's how important it is to be shaped by God's wisdom and God's truth, and not the truth of the world. In so many ways, the disciples are setting the course, not just for the next days or weeks of their ministry together, but for the next, larger season as well.

Look at what Jesus says in verses 1 and 2: "Don't be troubled. Trust in God. Trust also in me. My Father's house has room to spare. If that weren't the case, would I have told you that I'm going to prepare a place for you?"

This is just one example. He's giving an immediate illustration of what it means for us not to be troubled. The idea of what waits for us in heaven is not the primary point of the passage. But Jesus says, "I made you this promise, and if I've made you this promise and I've told you that this is true, and if you believe me in this, then you should believe me in all things." In other words, to find wisdom and truth begins with a certain, critical element of faith. "When I go to prepare a place for you, I will return and take you to be with me so that where I am you will be too. You know the way to the place I'm going" (vv. 3-4).

Now, I love Thomas. Thomas is one of my favorite disciples because he and I are a lot alike. I am eager to say the first thing that comes to my mind—too eager, many of my friends would say. I remember saying in a sermon once, "Like Thomas, I probably would've asked to see Jesus' wounds and scars too." This woman on the front row looked as though she were on the verge of a stroke or a heart attack. But I was serious; I meant it. I like empirical data. That's just how I am wired. I understand what Thomas is struggling with. He's honest and says what he's thinking. It doesn't mean that Thomas doesn't believe what Jesus is saying; it just means that he is relying way too much on his own wisdom and his own version of truth to define his next steps. Once he agrees to follow (such as in John 18 and during the death of Lazarus in John 11), Thomas will go deep into the fire. But deciding to follow requires moving out of his comfort zone first, and that is never simple.

> Thomas asked, "Lord, we don't know where you are going. How can we know the way?"
>
> Jesus answered, "I am the way, the truth, and the life. No one comes to the Father except through me. If you have really known me, you will also know the Father. From now on you know him and have seen him." (John 14:5-7)

I love this interchange, because it's one of the most important theological interchanges in Scripture. "How are we to know the way to new life?" Thomas asks. This is it, the crossroads between human intellect and God's truth. What Jesus says next is at the heart of all that he has preached and that for which he ultimately will give his life. I can't help thinking that Jesus wants to answer, "Thomas, do you know how long I have prayed for your eyes to open enough to ask this question? Thank you, Thomas, for asking that question." But Jesus simply responds, "I am the way, the truth, and the life. No one comes to the Father except through me." I love the way God works. He's not going to ask something of us where he has not provided the information we need or already modeled the answer for us—and most times, he has done both at the same time.

If the conversation had ended here, it would have been a great lesson in mentorship or theological modeling. But the conversation continues with an exchange between Jesus and Philip that establishes why what Jesus has intended and has prayed for the disciples is more than words. Jesus intends that his disciples will have wisdom and truth, but these things can come *only* from relationship with the Father. It was easy in the Greek world to philosophize religion into principles and learning points. But this had nothing to do with the classroom or rote learning. Jesus was talking about wisdom and truth that came to life in our relationships and did more than feed us knowledge; they transformed the soul. Truth was more than knowing; it was real transformation.

Along comes Philip. This scene seems somewhat anticlimactic after the first two interactions. But that appears to be the purpose.

> Philip said, "Lord, show us the Father; that will be enough for us."
>
> Jesus replied, "Don't you know me, Philip, even after I have been with you all this time? Whoever has seen me has seen the Father. How can you say, 'Show us the Father'?

Don't you believe that I am in the Father and the Father is in me? The words I have spoken to you I don't speak on my own. The Father who dwells in me does his works. Trust me when I say that I am in the Father and the Father is in me, or at least believe on account of the works themselves." (vv. 8-11)

I remember our youth minister reading this passage to us when I was just a young student. I got so confused. But in simple form, this is what Jesus is saying: "If you're watching me, Philip, you see the Father; and if you want to see the Father, all you need to do is watch me. That's all there is to it." That's the exchange. It is very simple and doable, Jesus is telling the disciple. And yet, maybe it is too simple—so simple that it stretches our wisdom and intellect to search for more. But there is no "more"—there's no more room for our simple intellect to conceive of what God is saying and doing. No, to capture what God is saying requires tapping into God's wisdom, not our own.

I assure you that whoever believes in me will do the works that I do. They will do even greater works than these because I am going to the Father. I will do whatever you ask for in my name, so that the Father can be glorified in the Son. When you ask me for anything in my name, I will do it. (vv. 12-14)

40

Our will must be aligned with God's will, and that happens only when we are in an authentic relationship with God. The first prayer of Christ we discussed is critical, because "fellowship with God" ultimately provides the foundation for the next step in our transformation through Christ. But Jesus is saying that too often our will is shaped by the truth of the world, instead of the truth of the Word. And therefore, too often when we ask God for assistance or guidance, we ask out of our own personal needs or desires. This is a calamity in the making, especially when our world begins to shatter or shake.

> If you love me, you will keep my commandments. I will ask the Father, and he will send another Companion, who will be with you forever. This Companion is the Spirit of Truth, whom the world can't receive because it neither sees him nor recognizes him. You know him, because he lives with you and will be with you.
>
> I won't leave you as orphans. I will come to you. (vv. 15-18)

What's the scariest feeling in the world? To feel abandoned? Alone? In John 14:15-18, Jesus clearly tells us, "If you follow the wisdom of the world, at some point, you're going to feel like an orphan"—a loneliness that permeates everything we are. And Jesus reiterates that the world will always abandon you in your most critical moments of need. However, at just the right moment, Jesus counters that his wisdom, his truth, will never leave us lonely. "Soon the world will no longer see me, but you will see me. Because I live, you will live too" (v. 19).

I've thought a lot about what it means to be shaped by God's truth. God has allowed me to go in so many different directions in my life. Some fit perfectly within God's will for my spiritual journey. Others—well—played perfectly into my weaknesses and selfish ways.

There's a story about a preacher who preached an entire sermon using a peanut to explain each biblical passage. The preacher explained, "I had run out of ideas, and I didn't know where to go. I saw a peanut on the counter one day, and I thought, *You know, I believe I can use that peanut to describe that biblical truth.*" He later recalled how a kid came up to him after the sermon and said, "You know, Preacher, I never thought I could learn that much from a nut!"

Now, before you think, *I learn from a nut every week at my local church*, I want you to think about the number of people to whom we listen every day in our lives. We listen to all kinds of people in this world. Some of them have the stamp of authority and leadership. Others have only the distinction of being the loudest voice in the room. And, yes, others are just plain ol' nuts.

Of course, the most important questions are: to whom

are you listening? and, where is your source of wisdom? Jesus would say that if your source of wisdom and truth is found anywhere other than in relationship with the Father, then you are missing not only the mark but also the *point* of the mark as well.

Following Something

A couple of years ago, I underwent forty-four weeks of treatments for a serious liver condition. The treatments were long and difficult. My wife was a wonderful support, and the countless friends and family members made the difference for me between surviving and overcoming. But the treatments also came with significant side effects. One of those was random anxiety attacks. These attacks came out of nowhere, and there were only a few signs for identifying them far enough in advance to help with any response. I had only a few signs, and they, in and of themselves, only made me more anxious as I awaited the results that would follow. Therefore, I would get more anxious while waiting to *get* anxious. That's pitiful, I know. One suggestion that really helped me came from my middle daughter. She is an avid Scripture reader. She suggested that when I felt the attacks coming on, I could "Scripture bob." This is the process of saying a quick prayer for God's guidance to lead you to open your Bible to the exact place from which you need to hear. So I took her advice. The results? The vast majority of the time, I went exactly to the place in the Bible where God's wisdom was strongest and right on par for me. The other few times I felt this method wasn't helpful were mostly when I was testing God more than seeking after his will.

I realized over the course of that year of treatments that so much of how God works in us truly happens in the one square foot of real estate just above our necks. Just as we can talk ourselves into so many broken places in our lives, I believe Jesus would say that we also can position ourselves for taking hold of God's wisdom and truth that will not abandon us at our greatest points of need. Jesus prays to the Father, "Father, do not let them listen to that voice that leads them far from you. No, let them trust in your voice. You've given them to me, Father, so they can hear you and follow me" (John 17, paraphrased). It is a beautiful and critical interchange between the Father and the Son.

We are all following something. I am a firm believer that there is very little in this world that is actually original. That's why when you hear names like Aristotle, Plato, Augustine, Marie Curie, and Steve Jobs, you know that those are special names. They've thought something or done something that is unusual and unique to their generation. Philosophers will tell you that most of what we know in this world is not original. We're all being shaped by our past. We're all learning from someone who's gone before us in our life. Jesus says, "I want you to learn from me. I want you to keep your eyes focused on me."

Who are *you* learning from? That's a huge question. Please don't just read it and move on too quickly. The answer to that question may be one of the most important pieces of information in your life—and not just for you. Remember what we discussed in the last chapter? We're all being mentored and shaped by something or someone, but there's also another side to that understanding: You are also shaping someone else. It may be your children, a niece or nephew, your best friend, the person sitting across the cubicle from you at work, or the person across the McDonald's counter from you. Wherever and whomever it might be, we are being shaped and also shaping someone else. We become the very wisdom we seek and crave through our words, our deeds, or our attitudes. That's why Jesus says, "I am the way, the truth, and the life" (John 14:6). You can't do it through any other person or process. That doesn't mean your religion is a bad thing or that other religions are bad things—they're just not going to lead you to the truth that is found in Jesus. And that truth, that salvation, that way to the Father is the ultimate source of salvation and eternal life. Period. And as Jesus would add, "I don't want you to miss that."

In the Gospels, Jesus prays for several very specific things, and each of his prayers contains a principle that will help us take hold of God's wisdom and guidance in our lives. The encounters in John 14 and 17 are the living out of those prayers.

Discovering Our Point of Reference

The prophet Jeremiah pleaded with Israel: "Please find what is your truth—you're going in the opposite direction of what God is calling you to do." (See, for example, Jeremiah 2.) We hear time and time again in the sermons of Paul, and again in the sermons of Jesus: "I am your point of reference." (See, for example, Mark 8:34; John 8:12; 14:6; 1 Corinthians 11:1.) What is your *point* of reference today?

I love lighthouses. The mission center that we started in the church I founded many years ago was called the Lighthouse. We named the center the Lighthouse in memory of the father of the family who donated the property. He had died tragically, in a house fire. The only item saved was a boxed, framed picture of a beautiful Maine lighthouse that had meant a great deal to the man's family when he was a child. The lighthouse was always a symbol of something bigger and safer, even in the center of a great storm.

What is your lighthouse today? When the storms are raging and you find yourself unsettled, what is your lighthouse? A lighthouse is a point of reference that points to safety at the

Now I'm coming to you and I say these things while I'm in the world so that they can share completely in my joy. I gave your word to them and the world hated them, because they don't belong to this world, just as I don't belong to this world. I'm not asking that you take them out of this world but that you keep them safe from the evil one. They don't belong to this world, just as I don't belong to this world. Make them holy in the truth; your word is truth. As you sent me into the world, so I have sent them into the world. I made myself holy on their behalf so that they also would be made holy in the truth.

John 17:13-19

center of the storm in your life. We may not always see it, but when we do, it is enough to point out the danger and save our lives.

There's a story about the captain of a battleship who sees a light in the distance. The captain sends out a message in that direction: "You need to shift ten degrees to the south." And a reply message comes back, saying, "You need to shift ten degrees north." The captain is incensed by this, and he sends out a second message that says, "I am the captain, and I order you to shift ten degrees south." The reply comes back, "I am Seaman First Class Jones, and I need you to shift ten degrees to the north." The captain is getting very angry by now, so he says, "I'm a battleship. I won't tell you again—go ten degrees south!" And the reply message comes back, "I'm a lighthouse. You have no other choice. Go ten degrees north!"

Your point of reference—what you are keeping your eye on—is incredibly important in this world.

Discovering What Anchors Our Wisdom

There are several different times in Jesus' teachings where he says, "Follow me," "Watch me," or "Do what I'm doing." These are anchor points for Jesus' teaching and the purpose in his ministry.

There's no better example of these anchor points than in

the first verses of Matthew 5. They're called the Beatitudes. I believe the Beatitudes are more than just great slogans on a keychain or a bookmark. I believe they are the anchors to Jesus' teaching ministry. And I repeatedly encourage people to go to the Beatitudes, to learn them and memorize them, because they are more than just beautiful poetic sayings.

From the moment Jesus begins sharing the Beatitudes, the reader knows they are important. The first words of the passage ascribe such importance to them: "Now when Jesus saw the crowds, he went up a mountain. He sat down and his disciples came to him. He taught them, saying..." (Matthew 5:1-2). In Jesus' day, whenever a prominent teacher would teach, he would find a high place from which to speak. There were no auditoriums or speaker systems. So the speaker would find the best place for projecting his teaching out to the gathered crowd. Also, once the teacher found a place from which to teach, he would sit down, signifying that what he was about to do was important. Jesus did both of these. What followed were the anchors for Jesus' teaching. Notice what Jesus says are his truths—the anchors of his wisdom:

Blessed are those who have utter dependence upon God. Blessed are those who love unconditionally. Blessed are those who give the benefit of the doubt. Blessed are those who seek justice and holiness. Blessed are those who walk humbly in the purpose that God has given to you. Blessed are those who live purely. Blessed are those who don't just love peace—they make peace in their life. Blessed are those who stand firm in their faith. (The Beatitudes, paraphrased)

Jesus believed that these truths and this wisdom framed the central values associated with following him. He goes on to say, in the verses immediately following the Beatitudes, that if you live these principles, you will be like salt to a tasteless generation, and light to a dark world (see Matthew 5:13-16). Those are pretty powerful descriptions! But that's how powerful the wisdom and truth of God are in Jesus. These truths infect you, change you, and transform you—they are that powerful. But Jesus says that you've got to *want* that level and that depth of wisdom and truth to come to life in you.

I love the story of Socrates and the young, pompous would-be student. (Socrates was one of the great thinkers of history.) This arrogant youth comes up to Socrates and says, "O great teacher, I want knowledge." Socrates replies, "Why don't you come with me?" He doesn't really like this guy on the front end, so he takes him to the ocean, walks him out into the water, and asks, "What do you want?" The young man answers, "I want knowledge, O great Socrates." Then Socrates grabs him and pushes him under the water for thirty seconds.

When he brings the young man back up, he asks him, "What do you want?" The young man responds, "I want knowledge, O great Socrates." Immediately, Socrates grabs him again and holds him underwater, for forty seconds this time. The guy comes up, a little bit shaken now, thinking he's with a crazy man, and Socrates again asks, "Son, what do you want?" Once more the young man answers, "I want knowledge, O great Socrates." Socrates pushes his head under the water yet again and this time holds him there for fifty seconds. Finally, Socrates pulls him back up and says, "Son, what do you want?" And this time, the young man replies, "I want air!"

Read again from the Beatitudes above—particularly what Jesus says about justice and righteousness. Here's the difference between how Jesus sees wisdom and truth, and how the world defines it. The world says you really ought to volunteer. You ought to learn to do some good things. But ultimately, you should get all that you deserve in life. Sure, it's fine to give to a good charity and to make some donations or do some good deeds. But ultimately this is about *you*.

You know what Jesus says to that? He says, "I want you to hunger and to thirst after righteousness and for justice and for doing good the way a hungry man who hasn't eaten in weeks is hungry, and the way a thirsty man who hasn't had a drink in days is thirsty" (see vv. 6-7). There is a difference. That is more than a good volunteer or a nice donation; that is a person who wants *air*. That kind of wisdom and truth changes not just your heart for the world—it changes your heartbeat for the next moment. What is the heartbeat of *your* truth? What is the foundation for your wisdom today?

In the Book of James, we read:

> Are any of you wise and understanding? Show that your actions are good with a humble lifestyle that comes from wisdom. However, if you have bitter jealousy and selfish ambition in your heart, then stop bragging and living in ways that deny the truth. This is not the wisdom that comes down from above. Instead, it is from the earth, natural and demonic. Wherever there is jealousy and selfish ambition, there is disorder and everything that is evil. What of the wisdom from above? First, it is pure, and then peaceful, gentle, obedient, filled with mercy and good actions, fair, and genuine. Those who make peace sow the seeds of justice by their peaceful acts. (3:13-18)

In case you missed what James said about real "wisdom from above," there were eight parts. This kind of wisdom requires that we:

1. have utter dependence on God,
2. have unconditional love,

52

3. give the benefit of the doubt,
4. seek justice and holiness,
5. walk humbly for God's purpose in our lives,
6. live purely,
7. make peace, and
8. live sacrificially.

There are no coincidences in God's Word. These eight parts also correspond to Matthew 5. They are a different version and wordplay than what we find in the Beatitudes, but they express the focus of each one. Scripture does this, clarifying one truth with references in other places. This reminds me that the Logos moves with purpose and presence throughout the entire Scriptures. Jesus embodies it, offers it, prays for it.

Discovering That Real Truth Equals Action

We can know all the knowledge of this world, and be filled with the many good things that Jesus has told us, and *it doesn't mean anything unless we are willing to faithfully live it out.*

One of Martin Luther's favorite quotes asserts that faith is found at the pronoun level of our language and experience. It reads: "He [Christ] died for me. He made His righteousness mine and made my sin His own; and if He made my sin His own, then I do not have it, and I am free."[1]

I never really understood Luther's sentiment until a friend put it into practice for me. Real wisdom is not just saying that Jesus is a great teacher; it's saying he's *my* teacher. He's not just a prophet; he is *my* prophet. He's not just the Lord, the Savior; he is *my* Lord, the Savior.

Think of it this way. The woman sitting next to me is *a* wife. Now, consider again: The woman sitting next to me is *my* wife. Is there a difference? You bet there is. And I am not the same because of it.

What is your source of guidance? What is your light-house? What is your point of reference? Wisdom is not easy. Truth is not simple. That is why Jesus prayed not only that we would have both, but also that we would have *the right kinds* of both.

My family and I went to the mountains a few weeks ago and visited an artisan camp. One of the cabins there had a room where they show you how to make maple syrup. Honestly, I didn't get up that day wanting to know how to make maple syrup—I just took a wrong turn on the way to the rest-room. However, I found myself in the workshop, unable to get out, and I didn't want to say, "No! I don't want to learn how to make maple syrup!" The teacher was a large man, and he seemed very intent on teaching me how to make maple syrup.

But while I was in there, God did something amazing. I

did not realize that when they make maple syrup, they first just fill up the buckets with the sap that comes out of the trees, and it is as useless at that point as anything you could possibly imagine. But they then heat up the sap, boil it, separate the water from the contents, and allow the sugar residue to concentrate. The syrup makers will then put the contents through several processes of heating and cooling, again and again. It takes a lot of time and work. But do you know what happens after all that work is done? You have something sweet, beautiful, and amazing: You have maple syrup.

Jesus is the way, the truth, and the life, and that "way" required a cross. Sometimes it still does, for you and me. But Jesus will not ask us to follow him to a place or through a difficult moment where he has not already been. Sometimes that kind of wisdom requires treatments and difficulties and mourning. Sometimes that sort of truth requires doing the hard things.

Sometimes following Jesus requires keeping our eye on the ball, and at other times it means closing our eyes and letting him guide us in the dark places. Still other times, it means knowing the difference between what we claim to have as important markers for our faith and life, and those gifts we truly possess that come only from God. Several years ago, I wrote a chapter for one of my books titled, "Having everything, possessing nothing." The point was that the world can convince us that we "have" lots of valuable things, when, in actuality and measured against the economy of what God says truly matters, we realize that no matter what we "have" of the world, we possess very little of importance.

Many times, faith requires more than we have, but it will never require more than we possess. If we are counting only on our natural abilities, strengths, or human gifts to make it, we will often be disappointed. But remember: God will never ask more of us than we truly "possess in him." Sure, sit back and try to soak in that distinction. It matters. And of course, in the end, I believe it is more than worth it. Getting this difference right changes us. That is why, when Jesus took time to be alone with the Father, he prayed for us, that we might receive real wisdom—the kind of wisdom that comes only from the Father and offers a sense of guidance and direction where no maps (or human intellect) will do.

Through the power of God's presence in Jesus Christ, wisdom comes to life in you. It doesn't express itself just as an intellectual quality or a personality trait. No, the wisdom of God that helped form all of creation into being unfolds inside our growing understanding of God's person and place in our time and space. That is why I believe God's truth in Jesus still sets us free. Not because wisdom ever disappeared or went missing, but because Jesus' prayer for wisdom in and through us deeply shapes the parts of us that the world cannot reach. But it becomes truth only if we are willing to believe it and live it—to make it as personal as the next breath we take.

Again, echoing Martin Luther's sentiments about the rather simple-looking, but cosmically large difference between calling Jesus "the Lord" and realizing and professing Jesus as "our Lord," we cannot fathom (even at only the most elementary of levels) the gift of God's granting us a glimpse of God's wisdom for our journey. In essence, we can talk about Jesus all day, but it is when he becomes our Lord that abstract faith conversations become a dialogue between the Creator and you. That is deeper than any Moralistic Therapeutic Deism; it is the persons of the Trinity stepping into the very center of your life's values, mission, purpose, and practice, and setting up shop.

*W*hen Jesus finished saying these things, he looked up to heaven and said, "Father, the time has come. Glorify your Son, so that the Son can glorify you. You gave him authority over everyone so that he could give eternal life to everyone you gave him. This is eternal life: to know you, the only true God, and Jesus Christ whom you sent. I have glorified you on earth by finishing the work you gave me to do. Now, Father, glorify me in your presence with the glory I shared with you before the world was created."

John 17:1-5

Prayer Focus 3

JESUS PRAYS FOR OUR UNITY

John 17:1-26

The third prayer focus of Jesus is where Jesus asks the Father to provide "unity" for his followers. Over the course of my ministry, congregations I have served have spent a great deal of time talking about "working together." We may not always speak directly to the issue, but each of the church's ministries takes people working together to accomplish the church's goals. I would bet that 99 percent of all ministries and programs require people working together. It takes more than just great teams of professional staff—it also takes lay leaders and volunteers working in unity to address both the simple and the complex ways of sharing the gospel. Peter Drucker, an expert in managing organizations, taught for many years that an organization could have great leaders but not the right team serving with them. Great vision is vulnerable to the level of unity among those charged with sharing that vision with the world.

People can put together great teams of individuals, but if those individuals do not learn to work together for one great cause, they never reach their goal. Jesus prayed in John 17 that the Father would build a church of great leaders, both staff and lay, professionals and nonprofessionals, who were unified behind a common vision. Jesus went on to assure us that such vision is found nowhere except in listening to and following the heart of God. Read John 17:1-26 (the entire chapter). I believe this is one of the most undervalued passages in Scripture. It's a long passage, but it reaches directly and deeply into the heart of the believer—we are nothing unless we learn to unify ourselves with the Father and Son, and take that unity as the foundation of our work with our brothers and sisters as well.

When Jesus finished saying these things, he looked up to heaven and said, "Father, the time has come. Glorify your Son, so that the Son can glorify you. You gave him authority over everyone so that he could give eternal life to everyone you gave him. This is eternal life: to know you, the only true God, and Jesus Christ whom you sent. I have glorified you on earth by finishing the work you gave me to do. Now, Father, glorify me in your presence with the glory I shared with you before the world was created.

"I have revealed your name to the people you gave me

from this world. They were yours and you gave them to me, and they have kept your word." (vv. 1-6)

We usually give the disciples a hard time through most of Scripture; so often, they seem to miss the point of Jesus' message completely. But in this passage, Jesus is really trying to defend them and offer them sincere, authentic grace. Given what they have experienced in their brief time together, Jesus is suggesting that they deserve at least *some* benefit of the doubt. Doesn't that sound nice? Have you ever needed an extra dose of benefit of the doubt? I certainly have! Look at what Jesus says next:

> Now they know that everything you have given me comes from you. This is because I gave them the words that you gave me, and they received them. They truly understood that I came from you, and they believed that you sent me.
>
> I'm praying for them. I'm not praying for the world but for those you gave me, because they are yours. Everything that is mine is yours and everything that is yours is mine; I have been glorified in them. I'm no longer in the world, but they are in the world, even as I'm coming to you. Holy Father, watch over them in your name, the name you gave me, that they will be one just as we are one. (vv. 7-11)

Think about that. The Son of God is talking about this identity that's been given to him by the Father, and through his prayer, the Son is saying to the disciples and to his future followers (including you and me), "I'm going to give that identity to *you*." Jesus is in the middle of advocating for your place close to God. It goes back to what Jesus seemed to be saying earlier, in John 14: "You're no longer orphans, acquaintances, strangers; you are the family of God—my family. You are the children of God—my children. You are no longer abandoned or forgotten." (See verses 18 to 21.)

> When I was with them, I watched over them in your name, the name you gave to me, and I kept them safe. None of them were lost, except the one who was destined for destruction, so that scripture would be fulfilled. Now I'm coming to you and I say these things while I'm in the world so that they can share completely in my joy. I gave your word to them and the world hated them, because they don't belong to this world, just as I don't belong to this world. (John 17:12-14)

Now you may want to underline this and write out to the side, "But we are *in* the world." Jesus is very particular about this point: We may be *in* the world, but we don't belong *to* the world. This is not our final home; this is not our ultimate resting place; this is not the end of the journey. *But we are most definitely here, and we will have to deal with it.* And so, Jesus is praying that we will be equipped to do what he is asking the Father to give us strength to accomplish, and that we will be able to do our work while we are in the midst of a world that ultimately does not care about our well-being.

As it is outlined in Ephesians 4, the purpose of the church—and my primary job as pastor of my church—is to equip each member of my congregation as a disciple, and *then* as a disciple-maker, who then grows to be an equipper for someone else. That is the great cycle of the Great Commission, so it's very important.

> I'm not asking that you take them out of this world but that you keep them safe from the evil one. They don't belong to this world, just as I don't belong to this world. Make them holy in the truth; your word is truth. As you sent me into the world, so I have sent them into the world. I made myself holy on their behalf so that they also would be made holy in the truth. (vv. 15-19)

Jesus is saying, "I have kept relationship with you, Father," because all holiness is in proximity to God and to God alone. "I have stayed in proximity to God so that they will see that relationship in my connection to you, Father. As they have watched and as they remember our relationship, Father, they too will remember and then model that experience of holiness." It's a simple process: If you want to be holy, you have to be in proximity to that which is holy—God.

> I'm not praying only for them but also for those who believe in me because of their word. I pray they will be one, Father, just as you are in me and I am in you. I pray that they also will be in us, so that the world will believe that you sent me. I've given them the glory that you gave me so that they can be one just as we are one. (vv. 20-22)

This is a standard rule of biblical studies: If Jesus says it more than once, we probably ought to pay attention to it. And in three consecutive sections of Scripture here, he has focused on unity. That's how important this is to Jesus. Here we have three mentions on the same topic within twenty verses.

"I'm in them and you are in me so that they will be made perfectly one. Then the world will know that you sent me and that you have loved them just as you loved me" (v. 23). Every time I read this particular passage of Scripture, I pause and think, *Oh my goodness. Jesus is saying, "You know what? The Father wants to love you, Shane, the same way that he loves me."* Wow! I truly don't know how to respond to that! How powerful to think of that gift. So no matter what you did today; no matter what baggage you woke up with or carried into your place of work; no matter what mistakes you've made; no matter what you know or get right or don't get right and don't know; can you come up with any response to God's offer to love you the same way he loved Jesus other than, *Wow*? There are no prerequisites for this love from God other than keeping your eyes on Jesus and allowing him to transform your life as your Lord and Savior.

> Father, I want those you gave me to be with me where I am. Then they can see my glory, which you gave me because you loved me before the creation of the world.
>
> Righteous Father, even the world didn't know you, but I've known you, and these believers know that you sent me. I've made your name known to them and will continue to make it known so that your love for me will be in them, and I myself will be in them. (vv. 24-26)

What does this prayer of Jesus tell us about the heart of God? In an earlier chapter we talked about how God wants a relationship with you, so don't put this book down without first settling this question in your spirit. If you don't have a relationship with Jesus, ask yourself, *What is keeping me from being in relationship with God?* Jesus prays that God will have a relationship with you and with me.

We also discussed earlier how God wants to shape your life and your journey with his wisdom and truth, and not the wisdom and standards of the world. It doesn't matter how much knowledge you possess; truth and wisdom come from a different spiritual fabric.

However, Jesus' prayer focus on unity may be the most important we've discussed so far. The reason God is moving us forward in these conversations about Jesus' prayers is because Jesus knows that to have a relationship with the Father, and to be shaped by the Spirit, by the truth, and by the wisdom of God, all of that is for nothing if we are not unified and of one heart and mind—first with the Father, and then with one another.

Of course, of all the prayers, this one contains the truth that Jesus is trying to convey to his disciples more than any other message. The adversary is prowling the earth, looking to dismember what the body of Christ can become; that's clear and simple. And he doesn't need to destroy us. He doesn't need to rip us apart and make some huge spectacle out of it. The adversary only needs to distract us. He only needs to create a little fracture so that people begin to mistrust one another. Satan convinces us that what we have heard, believed, and trusted is not the truth. He only needs to get us disunified in some way that keeps us from reaching our potential in Christ.

I'm praying for them. *I*'m not praying for the world but for those you gave me, because they are yours. Everything that is mine is yours and everything that is yours is mine; I have been glorified in them. *I*'m no longer in the world, but they are in the world, even as *I*'m coming to you. Holy Father, watch over them in your name, the name you gave me, that they will be one just as we are one. When I was with them, I watched over them in your name, the name you gave to me, and I kept them safe.

John 17:9-12

And that's why in John 17, right before the Crucifixion, Jesus is not just praying for himself and for his disciples; he's also praying for everyone who believes (and, thus, who *will* believe) that *unity* will be at the center of their faith journey. Jesus knows that even today, the adversary is looking to create disunity and disconnection in our lives—in our churches, our marriages, our children, our parents, and our workplaces. At any place where Satan can cause a sense of disunity and unsettledness in our lives, he gathers an advantage.

For instance, consider Jesus' temptation in the wilderness (see Matthew 4:1-11; Luke 4:1-13). What are the things with which Satan tempts Jesus? First, Satan tempts him with the basic necessities. Second, Satan tempts Jesus in his ambition. But the last temptation may be the most important one, for this is where Satan asks Jesus, "Are you sure you can trust what the Father is saying to you?" The adversary is trying to create disunity between the Father and the Son. That is how important unity is in the body of Christ—Satan uses disunity even as a tactic in tempting Jesus in the wilderness. I have a friend who says that our greatest asset is the witness of our people when we are living as the body of Christ. But do you know what our greatest weakness is? When those same people are living disunified in our witness to Christ.

When nonbelievers' only experience of the church has

been Christians tearing each other apart and being petty, why on earth would they want to invest in something that looks so much like the rest of the world? Jesus knows that unity is important. Look at what he prays in the very first part of John 17. In praying for himself, he says to God, "My greatest strength is being unified in you." And then regarding his disciples, Jesus adds, "I know they're going to struggle with the next days and months of life," and he knows that every one of them will become a martyr except for John. Whether the disciples understood it at that point or not (and obviously, they *did not*), Jesus knew that unity would be their greatest strength in the future.

And that has not changed for us today as people following Jesus and looking to God for direction in our lives. Given the current state of the church and its constant fight over ideologies and human issues, the church looks awfully vulnerable to disunity and brokenness from within. Just as important as it was in Jesus' prayer two thousand years ago, our greatest modern asset is unity as well.

There are three things that I believe Jesus teaches us about unity. This unity is expressed in the covenant between God and us, and then also within our relationships together. In fact, the concept of unity is so important to our journey that when that covenant is out of balance, Scripture hints that the rest of life is out of balance too. In those situations, our first priority as individuals, churches, and partners along the journey should be to solidify our connection to God and to one another.

Unity Makes Us Safe, Strong, and Able

In John 17:11, Jesus says, "I'm no longer in the world, but they are in the world, even as I'm coming to you. Holy Father, watch over them in your name, the name you gave me, that they will be one just as we are one." Jesus seems to be saying that *we are safest, strongest, most able to face the struggles in this world when we are in unity with our brothers and sisters, and when we are in unity with Christ.* Unity is our protection against the difficulties of this world. Again, the most troubling result of disunity is a world that is out of balance for life.

One of my favorite sayings in ministry is, "I don't know anyone who gets up in the morning, looks in the mirror, and says, 'Today looks like a great day to screw up my life!'" But what I *do* see are people who get out of bed and make one decision that's not too good, which leads to a second decision, which leads to not-so-good third, fourth, and fifth decisions, leading then to a pattern of even worse decisions that dominate our futures. At this point, it is *not* unusual for a person to wake up, look in the mirror, and say, "How in the world did I screw up my life?"

Jesus knows that unity with the Father is critical to our

having unity with one another. Therefore, our devotional lives, our intentional prayer times with God, create more than just biblical knowledge; they also help us to create a connection with the Father that informs every other aspect of our journey. Personally, I cannot exist without my study and devotional time with Jesus. It is my lifeline to handle the struggles of this world. I am stronger in my mind, I am stronger in my relationships, and I am stronger in my body the more time I spend with Jesus. The time spent with God—and the time spent with friends, family, and colleagues—those moments of unity in the Word make me a stronger person for the journey.

How about you? Are you as strong as you should be for the journey? Or do you feel as if your life is coming undone?

I love the *Peanuts* cartoon where Lucy wants Linus to change the TV channel. Linus doesn't want to change it: "What makes you think you can walk right in here and take over?" Lucy holds up her hand: "These five fingers. Individually, they're nothing, but when I curl them together like this into a single fist, they form a weapon that is terrible to behold." After thinking it over for a moment, Linus responds, "Which channel do you want?" Then, turning away, Linus looks at his own five fingers and says, "Why can't you guys get organized like that?"[1]

There is nothing that the body of Christ can't solve. And

there is nothing in this world that is unusable or without impact. But the church is often held back by simple, plain old fear. Fear of saying the wrong thing. Fear of what the next steps might cost us. Fear of what might be expected of us. Fear of what might be comfortable or uncomfortable. Jesus says, "You're not on this journey by yourself. Not only I am with you to the very end of the age, but you can also count on your brothers and sisters as well. Take up the mantle for each other. Stand in the gap for each other. Do more than claim faith in me; live your love for me by having love for one another. You're on this journey together." And although Jesus doesn't come out and say it directly, he insists to each of us, "If you will truly work together, you will not only drive away your fear but also change the world."

Unity Makes an Impact on Our World

If you want to see an impotent church that is not living up to its potential, find a church that is not unified. Churches without unity experience brokenness that transforms itself into pettiness. Nothing affects a church's unity like the simple presence of pettiness. It is a silent killer, because it masks itself with sarcasm, apathy, or "constructive criticism" that eats away at the health of the church from the inside. I tell my staff and lay leaders that there are two unwritten rules for the health of our church: (1) no pettiness, and (2) if you have to say something difficult, say it in love. If we can begin with these two basic rules in our relationships, we will be prepared.

But most of us do not live up to our potential. The reasons have little to do with training or skill; most people I know who have been raised for service and leadership in the church are qualified and prepared. Instead, Satan limits our effect as leaders and as servants in the body of Christ by fracturing our relationships in working with our brothers and sisters. It doesn't matter how gifted two people may be; if they can't work together, nothing gets done.

A dear friend of mine in Memphis, Michael Cody, is the former attorney general of the state of Tennessee. He had a stellar legal career. But probably most interesting is that he was part of the legal team that represented Dr. Martin Luther King and the Southern Christian Leadership Conference during the sanitation workers' strike in Memphis in 1968. Michael talked with Dr. King and several of his associates the day before Dr. King's assassination. Michael also was present at Mason Temple when Dr. King presented his famous "I've been to the mountaintop" sermon. While talking about those amazing and tragic days, Michael told me that Dr. King had been exhausted during the trip and had not planned to go to Mason Temple to speak on that fateful night. Dr. Ralph Abernathy and the team arrived at Mason Temple and realized the thousands gathered were there to hear Dr. King. Dr. Abernathy contacted Dr. King and told him he *had* to come to the temple. The people didn't *want* to hear Abernathy—or anybody else. They wanted to hear Martin Luther King Jr.[2] And that whole day, Dr. King had been trying to remove himself from the responsibility of that day's final commitments. Michael said it was easy to see that Dr. King was weary. Those previous days and weeks had been so difficult for him and his team. Literally, they were trying to be all things to all people.

But our opportunities for impacting our world do not run on our time. Those moments often come at the most inopportune junctions, and yet they also can provide for some of the most powerful results.

By the time Dr. King got to Mason Temple that evening, his exhaustion had anchored itself into his soul. Just listen to his words: "I may not get there with you. But...we, as a people, will get to the promised land!"[3] Dr. King's entire speech was about more than *physically* being present with one another; it was about being present with one another at a deeper place— one that changes each of us and everything around us. Jesus prayed that we would be united because he knew that is how we impact our world.

I have preached for more than twenty years that the best

way to change our world is to allow the church to be the church, together. I am not a fatalist when it comes to the church. I don't believe that an institution (no matter what you think of that word) exists for two thousand years for nothing. Yes, we have issues and deep problems, but we also possess a story and a narrative that draws back to the shores of the Sea of Galilee, to the Temple in Jerusalem, and to a hill named Golgotha. I believe there is no greater hope for the world than when the church is acting like ... well, *the church*—just as Jesus intended.

Jesus says if you want to make an impact in your life, go and be the church (see Matthew 28:18-20). Peter got up and preached the very first sermon after Jesus' death, and three thousand people joined the church. That's a good Sunday; I would be OK with that. And yet, I have also learned that I would be OK to live my whole life for just one soul to truly come to know Jesus as Lord.

The first great evangelism program was in Acts 2:42-47. The early church decided upon a trajectory of life that was revolutionary. They decided to allow the church simply to be the church. When people look at our churches today, do they go, "Wow! I want what they have"? They may not know much about church doctrine; they most likely haven't read your church's mission statement; they probably haven't heard a single sermon I've preached; but chances are they *have* seen you and me—how we treat one another and our world. Jesus says that is enough to paint a picture for a nonbeliever (see John 13:35). Paint a faithful picture, and we impact our world forever.

A report of the Memphis Ministers Association states that in Memphis, where I live, there are approximately seven hundred thousand people who do not go to church on a regular basis. And in a recent conversation of faith leaders in our city, it was stated that the number-one reason nonbelievers don't attend church is because of the witness of other Christians. But do you know what they agreed the number-one reason is for those who *do* attend church? You got it—it's the witness of other Christians. Let's put down our excuses and brokenness and walk toward the world together. That unity changes lives, beginning with our own lives first. Jesus says such unity impacts the world. (See John 17:22-23.)

Unity Glorifies God

In John 17:1-5, Jesus shows us that *we glorify God when we are unified.* If you want to bring shame on the gospel, then act like a church that is divided. If you want to bring sadness, if you want to bring tears to God's eyes, then be a church that is not connected to one another. Unity means that much to Jesus.

Do you know the real reason why Jesus was weeping at

Lazarus's tomb? It wasn't because Lazarus was in the tomb; Jesus had already raised two people from the dead. And, as some modern scholars have suggested, it wasn't because his friend had died. Instead, Jesus was upset with the others around the tomb who were perfectly alive but walking around as if they were already dead (see John 11)! The scene was traumatic, even for Jesus. The mourners at the tomb were fussing and fighting with one another over the smallest of issues, such as the gossip over why Jesus had not come more quickly and what Jesus' relationship with the family truly was. Here, in the midst of what would become one of the great miracles of the New Testament, the bystanders missed the unfolding power of God in front of them. And therefore, as Scripture describes, Jesus saw this disunity of faith and purpose, and he wept.

I believe Jesus weeps every time he looks at a church that is fighting among itself. Jesus knows that disunity is one of the adversary's favorite and best weapons against the church. In fact, we must always be prepared for Satan, whom Scripture tells us is seeking to distract and destroy us by separating us from God and from one another. (See Luke 22:31–32 CEV.) When we remain unified, connected in our goal to live as the body of Christ, we not only keep the church strong and on focus; we also impact our world. Unity brings glory to God.

I had an uncle whom everyone in the family said was "a bit

crazy." I loved him, but he was just always "around the bend," if you get the picture. Now, my uncle was always a gentle soul and was one of the most sincere animal lovers I know. But his love for animals developed, he said, from "not being very loving to them as a child." In fact, he told me that when he was a little boy, he liked to take two cats and tie their tails together. His description of the confusion that followed, when those cats tried to free themselves from each other, provides some of the most memorable and disturbing images I can imagine. Now, no one should ever do such a thing. However, as I think about the scene unfolding, the entire illustration reminds me that you can, indeed, have union without unity. I believe those cats would be the first to testify to that.

Think about that for a second. We are tied to a lot in this world. But we are often not unified. I got to see an example of union coupled with unity last night. My daughters did a beautiful dance at their annual recital. They have been doing ballet for years, and as I watched them dance last night, it occurred to me that all three of them are talented in their own right. They practice several days each week, and they love dance to their core. As individual dancers, they are skillful and talented. But aside from their skill, preparation, and commitment, what made their presentation last night so beautiful is the fact that they did it in step together. Their individual gifts came to life exponentially as they combined their gifts and danced in unison with the music.

It reminds me of Psalm 87:7: "And while they dance, people sing: 'The source of my life comes from you.'" When people look at the dance of the church, or of you or me or any Christian believer, for that matter, I pray that the first thing they say is, "Wow! Their joy must come from God," and that they will be amazed by how in step we are. What glory this will bring to God!

John Wesley, the founder of the Methodist movement, said, "I am not afraid that the people called Methodists should ever cease to exist. . . . But I am afraid, lest they should only exist as a dead sect, having the form of religion without the power."[4] As we understand from so many other examples of life, our world is filled with images of union, but that does not mean that we experience true unity.

Union without unity; there is a difference. Jesus prayed for unity among God's people.

*T*hose who love their lives will lose them, and those who hate their lives in this world will keep them forever. Whoever serves me must follow me. Wherever I am, there my servant will also be. My Father will honor whoever serves me.

"Now I am deeply troubled. What should I say? 'Father, save me from this time'? No, for this is the reason I have come to this time. Father, glorify your name!"

Then a voice came from heaven, "I have glorified it, and I will glorify it again."

John 12:25-28

Prayer Focus 4

Jesus Prays for Lives that Bring Glory to God

John 12:27-36

I preach nearly two hundred sermons each year. I try to be as prepared and focused as possible. Like many pastors, I like having my sermons "ready to go." Although I am fully aware of and encouraged by the intercession of the Holy Spirit, it still sort of unnerves me—just to be brutally honest. Of course, given the number of times that the Holy Spirit tends to intervene in my sermon prep, God doesn't seem to mind my angst. (You should envision a smiley face at this point.) But seriously, I want the sermon to be God's words, not mine. Ultimately, this is God's show (another smiley face)!

But as I think of what God is saying to us through the prayers of Jesus, I realize all the more that God's lessons for us are shaped by the power of our context, and thus we are constantly both in need of and blessed by the Holy Spirit's intercession. No one understands our need in this moment more than God. Thus, God's Word is not, and should not be, static. Quite the contrary, God's Word, two thousand years later, continues to move organically within our lives. God wants to change us, beginning from the inside out. God is not a distant deity, set apart on a mountain or behind a holy altar. No, as we have mentioned before, God craves a personal relationship with you and with me.

While our family was out to eat, my two oldest daughters, Sarai Grace and Juli Anna, got into a conversation about Reformed theology and such doctrines as "once saved, always saved"; nope, the Stanford family can't just have normal conversations about things. I remember thinking to myself, even in the moment, that what God was doing in that conversation was so new and so perfect. It's tied to this wonderful theological conversation that's been going on for millennia, and yet it comes to life because of these two hearts that want to know more about their God.

When Jesus is talking to his disciples, particularly in these passages in John, where he unburdens his heart, it isn't just about Jesus going with some cosmic plan. Jesus didn't have a manual that the Father sent with him from heaven that read, "OK, you need to teach them A, B, C, and D, and A is a little hard—you need to work on that one." It is about relationship and being personally connected in what God is doing even today through the Scriptures. As you read the key passage of Scripture for this chapter, John 12:27-36, be available to what God is saying to you, and know that although these words were written two thousand years ago, they can speak to you in your current moment and context as new and as powerfully as though he were writing them right now.

As Christians, we believe that the Scripture is not just a collection of holy words but rather holy words set within a sacred text meant to embody the very Spirit of God. So, unlike other holy religious works, the living "Logos" (or eternal Word of God) is meant to be alive, almost organic in nature. Thus, how that Word imprints itself upon our hearts may be as powerful as the words printed on a page.

Read John 12, beginning with verse 27. Most pastors preach around this passage because Jesus is talking about the Father's and his relationship more than he usually does here, and in an incredibly personal tone. But this passage, maybe more than any other, gives us a glimpse into what the prayers of Jesus tell us about the heart of God. Clearly, John 12 indicates that our lives should bring glory to God—in fact, Jesus specifically prays to the Father about one of his most personally difficult moments to come (see the prayer in the Garden), asking that God would be glorified. This wasn't some premeditated prayer, but the kind of prayer that rolls off the tongue without all of our senses fully engaged. In other words, the sentiments of John 12 are deeply emotional. So, "bringing glory to God" is much more than an important petition from Jesus. Jesus' prayer that his life would bring glory to God is meant to teach us something at a core level: our *own* lives should bring glory to God.

"Now I am deeply troubled," Jesus prayed. "What should I say? 'Father, save me from this time'? No, for this is the reason I have come to this time" (v. 27). In reality, this conversation should calm you. It should give you hope that the Son of God, who is more than aware of what's happening in our lives and what's about to happen in his, is still having this conversation. God knows what it's like to sit in your place. God knows what it's like to go through difficulties, to have relationships that are struggling. God knows this by making himself, as it says in Philippians 2, available to humanity, to be in our skin, to be incarnated. And Jesus says, "I could say, 'Deliver me,' but this is why I've come."

Then he says,

"Father, glorify your name!"
  Then a voice came from heaven, "I have glorified it and I will glorify it again."

The crowd standing there heard and said, "It's thunder." Others said, "An angel spoke to him."

Jesus replied, "This voice wasn't for my benefit but for yours." (John 12:28-30)

The reason Jesus is spending so much time sharing his personal emotions and pointing us back to the Father in his own prayers is so that we will understand what it's like to be unified in Christ. He wants us to know the power of what it means to have our lives shaped by God's wisdom, and not the wisdom of the world. He's showing us what it means for us to live lives that bring glory to God. "This is for your benefit, not mine," Jesus says.

"Now is the time for judgment of this world. Now this world's ruler will be thrown out. When I am lifted up from the earth, I will draw everyone to me" (vv. 31-32). This is important. You don't want to miss this. A lot of times in their sermons, preachers speak only about those who are drawn to the cross for salvation. That's not what Jesus is saying, though. He says, "Everyone will be drawn to me once the power of the cross is completely revealed in time." This means that all who have not followed the cross are going to have to stand accountable for how they deal with the cross—what that cross means to them, even if it means nothing. And Jesus is saying, you need to be ready for that as well.

(He said this to show how he was going to die.)

The crowd responded, "We have heard from the Law that the Christ remains forever. How can you say that the Human One [Son of Man] must be lifted up? Who is this Human One?"

Jesus replied, "The light is with you for only a little while. Walk while you have the light so that darkness doesn't overtake you." (vv. 33-35*a*)

To paraphrase Jesus' words: "You need to stay in the light as long as you can, because you will find yourself in darkness at some point." And that light is not going to be shining just for that darkness to experience it—it's going to be your salvation; it's going to be that reminder of not only where you're from, but also where you're going. And that is so important for us. Walk in the light while you can. "'Those who walk in the darkness don't know where they are going. As long as you have the light, believe in the light so that you might become people whose lives are determined by the light.' After Jesus said these things, he went away and hid from them" (vv. 35*b*-36).

So many people have tried to make something more out of this passage. You know what's happened with Jesus here? He has unburdened himself; he has poured himself out and said, "This is your life from here on out. Things are going to change, and I can't promise you that they're going to be easy or comfortable. That's why you need to walk in this light. You need to soak up this relationship with me as much as you can, because your journey is not guaranteed to be an easy one." Does that sound familiar to you? And he says, "I don't want you to be just those who have *learned about* the light; I don't want you to be just *students* of the light—I want you to be *children* of the light."

That's the first time in Scripture where Jesus characterizes the entire relationship with his people as something more than simply being a teaching-rabbi / learning-student relationship, instead equating it now with being as intimate as family. Here, he is saying, "You're my guys; you're my brothers; you're my family." And yet, Jesus then goes away, because in these next moments of his humanity, I believe Jesus did not know what would come next. Not that Jesus lost his power or his place as the Son of God—quite the contrary. This interaction modeled for Jesus exactly what you and I would go through, and the incarnation of Jesus was able to experience it completely. When you have uncertainty about what will happen next—when doubt begins to speak loudly—what happens? Well, for Jesus, teacher from Nazareth and Son of God, he went away to spend time with the Father, because he knew the strength he would need in the next moments would not be found in himself.

Now, some critics and theologians will want to fillet me

over the uncertainty and vulnerability that I suggest in the persona of Jesus. It sounds too risky and picks too close to his divinity. But imagine this—the God of the universe has already humbled himself to take on flesh, place, time, and circumstance. What could be more sovereign or divine than to embody also the very heart of our most fateful (and, yes, that is exactly the word I wanted to choose) moments. God embedded into the deepest places of humanity's fears and potential just so that a divine lesson about reaching back to the divine in times of trouble and uncertainty could be modeled without confusion. This illustration of Jesus' intentions for the disciples goes way beyond "This is what Jesus said to do..." It becomes *clearly* "Remember what he did?"

I don't know exactly where you are on your personal journey, but I know that many of us are going through times of great struggle. And I know that for some of us, we're wondering where the light is, because the world has seemed awfully dark. But I believe the light has not left you. And my prayer is that the people somewhere close beside you can be that light that can get you back to that path.

Now, if you feel you are not in that place and that right now everything is going pretty well, I want you to be conscious of this: you had better walk in the light while you can. It is so important that we take every opportunity to be in the presence of God. Do not miss an opportunity, a moment, to point your life back to God and to learn what he's trying to tell you. The prayer of Jesus reminds us that as God is shaping us, as God is unifying us, he's also building within us in every moment and at every opportunity a chance to bring glory to the Father.

John 15:1-17

The powerful shaping presence of God is found all over the mid to latter part of the Gospel of John. As we have read in John 12, the urgency with which Jesus preaches to his disciples about having a new relationship with God through Christ is almost palpable. He works so hard to prepare them for "the real world" and to shape them for their glorious-but-difficult time ahead.

However, Jesus retools the message a bit in John 15, reminding the disciples that the ultimate glue for their relationship with God and with one another is the love found in Christ. And the more the disciples can root themselves in the vine that is Christ, and the Father, the stronger their message and work will be. Of course, the by-product of all this work will be humility of spirit and grace that will transform the believer at a core level.

Thus, in John 15, Jesus says that the transformation of the believer brings, in that moment, a specific time of glory to God; but, without our ever really understanding it, it also develops an ongoing pattern of life that brings glory to God.

I am the true vine, and my Father is the vineyard keeper. He removes any of my branches that don't produce fruit, and he trims any branch that produces fruit so that it will produce even more fruit. You are already trimmed because of the word I have spoken to you. Remain in me, and I will remain in you. A branch can't produce fruit by itself, but must remain in the vine. Likewise, you can't produce fruit unless you remain in me. I am the vine; you are the branches. If you remain in me and I in you, then you will produce much fruit. Without me, you can't do anything. If you don't remain in me, you will be like a branch that is thrown out and dries up. Those branches are gathered up, thrown into a fire, and burned. If you remain in me and my words remain in you, ask for whatever you want and it will be done for you. My Father is glorified when you produce much fruit and in this way prove that you are my disciples.

As the Father loved me, I too have loved you. Remain in my love. If you keep my commandments, you will remain in my love, just as I kept my Father's commandments and remain in his love. I have said these things to you so that my joy will be in you and your joy will be complete. This is my commandment: love each other just as I have loved you. No one has greater love than to give up one's life for

90

one's friends. You are my friends if you do what I command you. I don't call you servants any longer, because servants don't know what their master is doing. Instead, I call you friends, because everything I heard from my Father I have made known to you. You didn't choose me, but I chose you and appointed you so that you could go and produce fruit and so that your fruit could last. As a result, whatever you ask the Father in my name, he will give you. I give you these commandments so that you can love each other. (vv. 1-17)

As you can see, the essence of bringing glory to God is found in our connection to God through Christ. Thus, our relationship, our guidance and wisdom, and our unity find expression as we work together in Jesus and bring glory to God.

We bring glory to the Father in three ways. Jesus wants us to experience and magnify each of these so that we recognize God's presence and also share it with everyone around us.

We Bring Glory to God Through Our Worship

The first way we bring glory to the Father is through our worship. And I'm not just talking about one hour on Sunday mornings. For Jesus, worship was any opportunity to be in the presence of the Father or to point others to the presence of the Father. And that's why he regularly had to take time away as a means of recalibrating his own spiritual compass.

Jesus was a faithful Jew. He went to the synagogue, and he participated in community and in the many rituals and festivals of his faith, such as Passover. He did all the things spiritually and religiously that he needed to do, yet he also understood that part of his worship was not just in his personal connection to God, but also with his brothers and sisters in connection to God. That's why gathering in community on Sunday mornings for worship, study, and fellowship is so critical for our lives. Remember what Jesus said: you're walking in the light so that when things are darker in your week, you will have a clear and focused reminder in your best path.

For so many of us, we see worship as something that we just check off the list. It happens at 8:30 or 9:45 or 11:00 on Sunday mornings. We go to church and listen to a sermon, or we might watch one online. But worship is so much more than that. My family and I can't make it in this world if our hearts and lives are not pointed back to God. And there are so many times when I point my life in so many directions other than toward the place that gives me the greatest strength and peace. Worship reminds me, time and time again, that God wants to work in those weaker places. Worship is our chance not just to offer our praise back to God, but to arrange our lives. How are you currently arranging your life? Worship is more than just one hour on Sunday mornings.

I'm not praying only for them but also for those who believe in me because of their word. I pray they will be one, Father, just as you are in me and I am in you. I pray that they also will be in us, so that the world will believe that you sent me. I've given them the glory that you gave me so that they can be one just as we are one. I'm in them and you are in me so that they will be made perfectly one. Then the world will know that you sent me and that you have loved them just as you loved me.

John 17:20-23

Recently I heard the story of a little boy who prayed at lunch one Sunday. The father asked his little son, "Would you say a prayer for us today? And remember to pray for good worship on Sunday." The little boy then prayed, "Oh, dear God, we had such a great time at church today. We just wish you could've been there with us!" It is a classic prayer and one that most of us have wanted to say many times for so many reasons. But what he meant was that he wished that God could've been there physically with them—he wished they could've reached out and touched God.

There probably are a lot of worship services we've been to where it's been a great time of performance or there's been some great teaching, but, just as the little boy offered, it would have been even better if we had allowed the full, palpable presence of Jesus to be there with us. Are we arranging our lives in worship to the point where right now, the closest experience and expression of God feels like the very next breath of your life?

We bring glory to God through our worship.

We Bring Glory to God Through Our Witness

I love what Matthew 5:15-16 says: "Neither do people light a lamp and put it under a basket. Instead, they put it on top of a lampstand, and it shines on all who are in the house. In the same way, let your light shine before people, so they can see the good things you do and praise your Father who is in heaven." The focus is not on the good works and not on the things you're going to do; it's on what rests at the center of your heart that causes you to do those things.

One of the ways you bring glory to the Father is through your confession. If someone put you on the witness stand and said, "OK, you've got a case to make here to prove your faithfulness to Christ, to prove that others should follow what you profess," is there enough evidence in your testimony to make someone want to believe your witness? For so many of us, it's not just that we don't have the works—we also lack an understanding deep inside of us of why our hearts should be transformed and our hands and feet should be more like those of Jesus.

Not long ago, I read *11 Indispensable Relationships You Can't Be Without*, by Leonard Sweet, an interesting postmodern theologian.[1] One powerful point from the book was the way he translates the word for *witness* out of the Greek as "withness." Dr. Sweet says this translation is so much more powerful because it goes beyond testifying about what we know of Jesus. That's the kind of witness God is talking about. We bring glory to God through our witness. Are we willing not just to confess Jesus as our Savior, but also to be with Jesus when things are not easy? Jesus is very clear that our "withness" is what will translate when other words and actions just won't do.

I read a statistic having to do with Jesus' interactions with others. The Gospels record 132 contacts that Jesus had during his ministry. Six of these contacts are in the Temple. Four are in synagogues. And the other 122 are out in the everyday mainstream of life.[2] I love the worship experiences at my local congregation. Our worship is powerful. All Christians need community. We need to sing the songs, read the Scriptures, lift our voices, pray, and study in our small groups. We need to be the hands and feet of Jesus. But more than that, worship comes to life most in the unexpected places, in the everyday mainstream of life. When you live your life faithfully, you bring glory to God. And usually, those moments of bringing glory happen in the places that are the farthest from our sanctuaries and worship centers. This is worship: wherever your "withness" begins.

We Bring Glory to God Through Our Works

Works. Now, before that word scares you, I am not talking about salvation or redemption. Works have no place in defining our eternal relationship with God. And yet, some of the most powerful sermons that will ever be preached won't have a single word attached to them. It'll be a cup of cold water, a touch for a grieving life, or putting your arms around someone who is lost and forgotten. I don't want you to miss this: What we do *as* Jesus is as important as what we do *for* Jesus in this world. It is the same in Scripture. How is your witness being lived out? Does what you do, and who you are when you are not in worship, bring glory to the Father?

And keep this in mind: There are going to be struggles. There always are. When you decide that you are going to point your life back to God—that you are going to make your worship a testimony, a "withness" to what Christ has done in your life, so that your every work and every deed becomes a way to worship him—not only will Satan notice; he will respond. But I cannot stress enough that Jesus didn't just say "Amen" in his petitions for our lives and future and hope for the best. No, he went to the cross for you and me. Jesus gave us the ultimate gift of prayer and worship, "withness," and serving.

I mentioned earlier some of my personal health challenges. In 2007, I had heart surgery on a 100 percent blockage. One of the physicians came up to me and whispered in my ear, "I'd like you to say a prayer for me right now." I'll just be honest: I thought, *I'm the one on the table; maybe today, you might pray for me.* The doctor could see from the look on my face that I was thinking, *Now?* And this is what he said next (I wrote it in my journal): "I heard you preach a sermon two years ago, and in it you said, 'It is when the night is the darkest, when the night is at its end, when our pain hurts the most and fear has its greatest chance to win, that we pray our loudest and our hardest—as C. S. Lewis says, not to change God, but to change us.'"

The doctor, even in that most unusual setting, wanted to know that I was willing to live what I professed. Because it wasn't about me; that was a chance to bring glory, even in that place, to the Father, to the One who carried me and who carries you in your place today. Wherever you may be right now, and in whatever struggle and whatever valley, what do people see when they see you? Do they see your struggle? Or do they see the One who overcomes the world for you in your struggle?

I remember hearing of a man at sea who was very seasick. If there is a time when someone feels he cannot do any work for the Lord, it certainly is *then*, in my opinion. While this man was sick, he heard that another man had fallen overboard. As he was wondering if he could do anything to help to save him, he got hold of a light and held it up to the porthole.

The drowning man was saved.

When the seasick man got over his sickness, he went up on deck and saw the rescued man. The saved man gave this testimony: He had gone down under the waves the second time, and was just going down again for the last time, when he put out his hand. Just then, he said, someone held a light to the porthole, and the beam from it fell on his hand. A man then caught him by the hand and pulled him into the lifeboat.

It seemed a small thing to do, to hold up that light, yet it saved a man's life. You don't need to do some great thing; you can simply hold the light up to the porthole for some poor, perishing soul who may be won to Christ and delivered to safety. Let us take the torch of salvation and go into these dark places, and hold up Christ to the people as the Savior of the world. Who knows? As we bring glory to God, imagine who might see your light shining brightly in the darkness and reach for salvation that changes them forever.

No one understood or preached this better than John Wesley. Read the words of his famous covenant prayer:

> *I am no longer my own but yours.*
> *Put me to what you will,*
> *rank me with whom you will;*
> *put me to doing,*
> *put me to suffering;*
> *let me be employed for you,*
> *or laid aside for you,*
> *exalted for you,*
> *or brought low for you;*
> *let me be full,*
> *let me be empty,*

let me have all things,
let me have nothing:
I freely and wholeheartedly yield all things
to your pleasure and disposal.
And now, glorious and blessed God,
Father, Son and Holy Spirit,
you are mine and I am yours. So be it.
And the covenant now made on earth, let it be
ratified in heaven.[3]

Indeed!

Recently my congregation has worked together through the twenty-four-week Covenant Bible Study. Covenant is a "walk through the Bible" study that fits the lessons and devotions around a discussion of covenant relationship and its presence in Scripture. It has been a great study, not just because of being able to draw closer to Scripture, but also because of the beauty of watching the body of Christ come together as well.

In John Wesley's sermons, most of which I have read, two major themes inspire me most. The first is the notion that God's Word allows us, together, to participate in the power and joy of salvation. We literally have a chance to tell "good news" to a world that desperately needs to hear it.

But the second major theme is the discussion found in

Wesley's Covenant Prayer—namely, that we would subjugate our personal wants and needs to live close to the heart of God. And in the process, as we draw closer to God, we draw closer to one another as well.

For the last several years, I have been asking a singular question in my devotional study at the end of each day: "What have I done today to bring glory to our holy, loving God?" Some days the answers are harder to find than on other days. But there are also those days when the answers are clear and wonderful, days when the Holy Spirit almost beats me to the punch, and I remember that particular interaction, that conversation, that act of kindness, or that moment of humble response when I believe that, just as God was "well pleased" with Jesus when he rose from the waters of the Jordan, God was "well pleased" with me. I can't describe what that feels like. It is not pride or self-congratulatory; instead it is a sort of "thank you" back to God for giving me a chance to be a part of what God is doing in this world. I never want that feeling to end.

Jesus knew that a life that brings glory to God is not a perpetual "self-award" moment but rather the most humbling truth we can experience—the understanding that the God of the universe decided to make covenant with you and me and then make us one.

Again, indeed!

*P*ray like this:

> Our Father who is in heaven,
>   uphold the holiness of your name.
> Bring in your kingdom
>   so that your will is done on earth
>   as it's done in heaven.
> Give us the bread we need for today.
> Forgive us for the ways
>   we have wronged you,
>   just as we also forgive those
>   who have wronged us.
> And don't lead us into temptation,
>   but rescue us from the evil one.

If you forgive others their sins, your heavenly Father will also forgive you. But if you don't forgive others, neither will your Father forgive your sins.

Matthew 6:9-15

JESUS PRAYS FOR OUR CONSISTENCY IN PRAYER (THE MODEL PRAYER)

Matthew 6:5-15

We've asked the question in every chapter: What is it that the prayers of Jesus are teaching us about the heart of God? In the first chapter, we learned that God wants to have a relationship with you. Next, we learned that God wants to shape your life and your path with his wisdom and direction. Following that, we learned that Jesus prays for unity among his followers. And in the last chapter, we talked about how important it is that everything we do and everything we are brings glory to God.

We have a little saying in our house when the kids are getting ready to go somewhere with someone else: "Don't embarrass the family!" Of course, they know we're kidding—sort of. But we want them to remember that everywhere you go, you represent the whole of the family—it's not just you representing yourself.

Jesus, in his prayers to the Father, is basically saying the same thing: "I pray for my disciples, for those you've put in my care, that they will bring glory to you in everything they do." And here's perhaps the most important part: Jesus prayed these prayers knowing all that would transpire over the coming days and weeks—that he would be abandoned, betrayed, and sent to the cross. Still, he prayed these prayers, even though he knew the horror of what the next part of the journey would bring. And that's why he was so fervent in his prayers to the Father. Jesus knew that ultimately all of his disciples (except for John, who would die a natural death on Patmos) would be asked to give their lives for him. Jesus knew that his disciples would need strength, hope, and God's presence more than humanly imaginable. And Jesus knew that as they lived faithfully through those difficult times, their struggles would bring glory to God and change the world. The prayers of Jesus are not benign words of encouragement. These are the final words before battle, before the jump, before racing out of the foxhole. Jesus prayed these prayers because he loved his followers, and because he loves you and me.

However, Jesus did not just want to pray *for* us. He wanted us to be a part of the prayers he was praying with the Father and to learn the nature of what communication between the Father and the Son meant. The words Jesus prays in Matthew

6 are the perfect example of Jesus teaching us about what being a part of the discipline of prayer should be. Known as the Lord's Prayer, these are not just a ritualized set of words that are easy to memorize and recite in worship. The Lord's Prayer is an outline, a glimpse into what *our* prayers should become as well. Jesus tells us that not only are we to "pray like this," but we are also to embody the nuances and deeper meanings of what each part of the Lord's Prayer says to us and for us when we use it in our spiritual journey. Let's take a deeper look at the Lord's Prayer.

"Pray Like This"

In Matthew 6:5-8, Jesus tells us,

When you pray, don't be like hypocrites. They love to pray standing in the synagogues and on the street corners so that people will see them. I assure you, that's the only reward they'll get. But when you pray, go to your room, shut the door, and pray to your Father who is present in that secret place. Your Father who sees what you do in secret will reward you.

When you pray, don't pour out a flood of empty words, as the Gentiles do. They think that by saying many words they'll be heard. Don't be like them, because your Father knows what you need before you ask.

The character of C. S. Lewis in William Nicholson's play *Shadowlands* said, "[Prayer] doesn't change God—it changes me."[1] God already knows what we need before we pray. We pray to alter our own wills so that they become aligned with the will of God. And so Jesus provides us an example of how we should pray that all we are called to do (and should want to do) in prayer has a framework. Jesus says:

> Pray like this:
>> Our Father who is in heaven,
>>> uphold the holiness of your name.
>> Bring in your kingdom
>>> so that your will is done on earth
>>> as it's done in heaven.
>> Give us the bread we need for today.
>> Forgive us for the ways
>>> we have wronged you,
>>> just as we also forgive those
>>> who have wronged us.
>> And don't lead us into temptation,
>>> but rescue us from the evil one.
>
> If you forgive others their sins, your heavenly Father will also forgive you. But if you don't forgive others, neither will your Father forgive your sins. (vv. 9-15)

Jesus is saying that when you adjust your prayer life to the will of the Father, you transform the whole of your spiritual life. After teaching us the outline of the Lord's Prayer, Jesus gives us this example of what such prayer and closeness means for the whole of what we do in God's name. You are in a different relationship than before—the stakes are higher once you are transformed in this new prayer relationship, because it's not about the words you're saying. Instead, it's about the relationship to which you have now committed and that you now have experienced.

I believe it is important to clearly examine and understand the Lord's Prayer to a point where it becomes more than just something you recite on Sunday mornings. The Lord's Prayer is meant to take on a transformational power in our lives, changing us from the inside out.

First, Jesus teaches in this passage that prayer is living and organic. It grows up inside of us. We shouldn't turn prayer into just a ritualistic part of our lives. But we also have to keep in mind that Jesus is *not* telling us we shouldn't pray every day or before meals or before bedtime. He's not saying that ritual is bad. But when the rituality of the prayer becomes the heartbeat of our prayer life, Jesus says, we become babblers in the faith. And between you and me, that just sounds really bad!

Remember: prayer is holy conversation between the Father

107

and Jesus. We are to model that conversation. The Lord's Prayer frames the conversation for us around the items Jesus does not want us to forget or lose. But Jesus is leaving it up to us to continue to fill in the blanks.

Preparing to Pray

First, before you pray, Jesus offers three pieces of advice—beginning points to guide and frame our prayer lives. He instructs us: "Go to your room, shut the door, and pray to your Father" (v. 6). This is one of the earliest occasions in Jesus' ministry where he calls the Father, who is God, *their* Father; that is, his hearers' Father, instead of just his own. Jesus has called him the God of heaven and the Father of creation. He has also referred to God as "*my* Father," in expression of the relationship between the Father and Jesus the Son. But only twice before this occasion has Jesus identified his Father as being "your" Father too. This is so important. These three things that Jesus does right off the bat signify for us that prayer is not meant to be a "recitation"; it's not just words; it is *who we are*—in our posture, our attitude, our expression, our burdens and baggage, and our hopes and fears.

My grandfather loved to say, "I am how I pray." He loved the Lord's Prayer. But he always realized that our prayer life is more than just what we write down or recite at the appropriate moments. It is an outflowing of who we are in Christ.

When you pray, don't be like hypocrites. They love to pray standing in the synagogues and on the street corners so that people will see them. I assure you, that's the only reward they'll get. But when you pray, go to your room, shut the door, and pray to your Father who is present in that secret place. Your Father who sees what you do in secret will reward you.

When you pray, don't pour out a flood of empty words, as the Gentiles do. They think that by saying many words they'll be heard. Don't be like them, because your Father knows what you need before you ask.

Matthew 6:5-8

Jesus' three quick rules for beginning to pray are telling. First of all, Jesus says, "Go to your room." This doesn't necessarily mean an actual, physical room. What Jesus means is that you must be intentional about your prayer life. It's not just something you can pick up on a Sunday morning or fit into a worship service. Every day should have an intentionality that combines real life with our prayers. "Go to your room." Go to a place that's set aside. Go to your moment of focus and quietude. Are you setting aside specific time to be in prayer and relationship with God?

Second, Jesus says, "Shut the door." This is an instructional time. Give it not just intentionality but also importance in your life. My prayer life has often seemed backwards, as though I am fitting prayer into life instead of my life into prayer. Jesus says, go to your room and shut the door on the world. Get rid of the distractions. Now, the apostle Paul tells us we are supposed to pray without ceasing (1 Thessalonians 5:17), and I'm not saying we shouldn't do that as well. But the Scripture also tells us that there has to be a time when we are so intentional that we shut the door on the distractions of the world. Is your prayer life that intentional as to be available for that kind of instruction?

Finally, Jesus says, "Pray to your Father." Your prayer life should not just be intentional or instructional; it also should be intimate. This is about a relationship between you and the Creator of the universe. This relationship is the doorway by which you enter into the presence of God, and there God entrusts you and your life with his own heart and will on a regular basis. Isn't that powerful? That's what Jesus says about prayer. Don't pray as the hypocrites do, or even as the priests do, only out of ritual awareness. Prayer, set within Jesus' framework, ultimately should change your life. Psalm 107:28-30 says it well:

> So they cried out to the LORD
>   in their distress,
>   and God brought them out safe
>   from their desperate circumstances.
> God quieted the storm to a whisper;
>   the sea's waves were hushed.
> So they rejoiced because the waves
>   had calmed down;
>   then God led them to the harbor
>   they were hoping for.

Do you want a prayer life like that? Do you want the seas to be hushed, the winds to be quieted, and for God to take you by the hand and usher you to that place of peace? That is the power of a prayer life—it is more than a collection of words to recite on a Sunday morning; it's more than just what we might read at the top of a devotional page. Those are all great, but God wants so intimately to be connected to you that every time you gather in prayer with God, something transformational and powerful can happen.

After Hurricane Katrina, I was working for the Mississippi Annual Conference of The United Methodist Church, and one of the areas where I was sent to help was the UMC district that included most of the Mississippi Gulf Coast churches. Katrina came aground at Gulfport, Biloxi, and Long Beach. I had never seen anything like it. But it was the personal encounters that affected me most. The devastation within two miles of the beach was unparalleled. And the personal stories of distress left me feeling as though I had a hole in my heart.

One story will stay with me forever. A large congregation from north Mississippi had been packing items such as water, food packets, and medical kits for families. The large availability of supplies meant the world to the people who needed them. But there were many specialized needs that could not be met as easily. One day, a young mom arrived at the relief area after having walked several blocks from what used to be her apartment complex. She was carrying her little baby, who was just a few months old. The woman had tears running down her face, and she said to the first relief worker she could find, "Sir, can you help me? I think my baby is dying." Her baby was suffering dehydration, severe diaper rash, and hunger. Water and other supplies were available, but there was nothing in that area for a small baby. Helpless, the woman asked if there were any baby supplies. The relief worker replied, "No. I'm very sorry."

By this time, between the cries of the child and the mother, the men and women at the supply truck also had begun to weep. One couple began to pray for the mother and her baby. There were no other options, it seemed. Just then, a man unloading supplies from the eighteen-wheeler cried out, "Look here!" He ran to the back of the trailer and held up two large packets of *new mother supplies*—including diapers, formula, diaper-rash cream, a new pacifier, and many other needed items. That day, no one doubted that prayer was a tangible part of faith, and not just mere words. The rejoicing took place for hours!

God's not playing with you. He didn't ask you to pray in order to keep you busy until something better came along. The prayers we pray can be life-changing and transformational. Now, not all our prayers are going to be answered like that. But remember that God is never *not* answering your prayer. He's just answering it based on what he knows the answer needs to be. When I go back and look at my own prayer journal, I see all the times God didn't necessarily answer a prayer the way I was wanting, but he was always answering—according to what was best for my life.

Jesus' Outline for Prayer

After getting ourselves prepared to pray, Jesus offers us another tool for developing our prayer life: an outline. The Lord's Prayer is the master outline for how and why we connect into the conversation between God, Jesus, and humanity.

I have prayed the Lord's Prayer every day of my life since I was sixteen, when I was asked to preach the youth revival in the church I was attending. The pastor invited me to join him each morning for a full week, to "pray up" for the revival. And I went. It was very early, and I was not a morning person. But rising that early simply to be in God's presence set a tone for me that I have kept for many years since.

When the pastor told me that we were going to pray for forty-five minutes to an hour, I was skeptical. I had never prayed that long. But beginning at 6:00 a.m. each day, we would take the Lord's Prayer from the King James version of the Bible and use it as an outline and a focus for our prayer time. The pastor taught me what I now believe is Jesus' gift to us in the Lord's Prayer. It is a living, almost-organic outline for how we can approach God and begin a conversation with him. We spent a few moments each morning reading through the entire prayer. The pastor then would break the Lord's Prayer into sections, and we would pray from there.

"Our Father, Which Art in Heaven, Hallowed Be Thy Name"

The first part of the Lord's Prayer places us directly in the presence of the Father. The beginning of our prayer life includes *praise*. We should take a moment in the presence of God to say, "Father, I am here! I don't understand everything you're saying to me; I don't understand everything I'm supposed to say to you, but I'm going to begin here, with praise." Psalm 95:2 says, "Let's come before him with thanks! Let's shout songs of joy to him." We begin with praise.

"Thy Kingdom Come. Thy Will Be Done in Earth, as It Is in Heaven"

The second part of the outline is, "Thy kingdom come. Thy will be done in earth, as it is in heaven." I call this the "holy humility" part of our prayer life.

Maybe this will explain better what I mean. For many years (and even occasionally now), my prayer life usually worked like this: "Help me, O God." Or, "O God, thank you for helping me." Those were basically the two parts to my prayer life. After praise, the next part in our prayer life should be holy humility:

"You know, Father, I don't know what you're calling me to do, but I pray that your will, just as it's done in heaven, will be done on earth in my heart. Begin with me, God."

But in order for this to happen, you have to humble yourself before the holiness of God. Before you make any requests, before you say anything else, you have to decide who's going to be in first place in your life. "Father, I want your will to be done, not mine." If you don't think this part of our prayer life with God is important, go to the garden of Gethsemane and listen to the prayer Jesus prayed to the Father (see Luke 22:41-46). Jesus knew all about holy humility, and he truly lived it out.

Does your prayer life have holy humility?

"Give Us This Day Our Daily Bread"

The third part of the outline comes after we have positioned ourselves humbly before God. Now we ask for *the basics and the necessities*; that is, the immediate needs in life. Nowhere in Scripture does it say that we are not to pray for what we need. Every day I pray that God will heal my body. Do I think that healing will take place the way I want it? Probably not. I may not be healed until I get face-to-face with Jesus. But I pray every day for that. I would be remiss if I did not pray for God to heal me. I pray for my healing within the context of the basic necessities of life. I pray for the resources my family needs. I pray for time, I pray for eloquence in order to communicate the things that are important in our lives, I pray for others, and I pray for the basic necessities in their lives as well.

Again, Scripture never says we shouldn't pray for our personal needs. But if we pray for those before we pray in holy humility, we get our priorities backwards. And the prayer says, "God, I need…" rather than, "God, give me what I need."

"And Forgive Us Our Debts, as We Forgive Our Debtors"

Think for a moment about what God is saying to us in this passage. You have to have certain things in your life, in your body, in your finances, if you are to make it in the world. There is nothing wrong with praying for the basic needs of life. But once you pray for those necessities, God says, then pray, "Forgive us our debts, as we forgive our debtors."

Dietrich Bonhoeffer, who would later be killed by the Nazis for his faith, said: "Judging others makes us blind, whereas love is illuminating. By judging others we blind ourselves to our own evil and to the grace which others are just as entitled to as we are."[2] The work of "unforgiveness" affects all of us. Bonhoeffer realized that no matter the treachery of the Nazis, he could not be held hostage by the kind of hate and anger that they bred inside those they hurt and wronged. That was evil's

117

worst effect—literally changing the victims' natures so that their pain and sorrow began to define them.

That's why forgiveness is such an important part of our prayer life. We live in an imperfect world filled with imperfect things that happen to imperfect people. We are not sanctified or fully perfected in our relationship with God yet, and we won't be until we are together on that heavenly shore. However, God transforms our earthly wounds into a strength that transcends the world's understanding.

Several years ago, I went through a very difficult betrayal in my life. Other than my health struggles, it was the most difficult moment of my life. I wanted to be so angry, and, of course, I wanted revenge. But the more I allowed those emotions to come to life in me, the more something inside of me died. I forgot how to show compassion, and I missed the small moments when God used brokenness to provide new understandings of his grace. Therefore, I came very close to giving in to my betrayal and anger. Luckily, God sent a dear friend to stand in the gap for me. That friend, mostly through prayer, showed me how to hand over my anger and also how to take responsibility for my part in hurting others.

This part of the Lord's Prayer so often is seen as a matter of asking the question, "How did you hurt someone's feelings today?" But it is so much more than that. Jesus knows that we often drag around the baggage of old burdens and hurts to the point where our spiritual walk becomes a limp, and we are no longer ourselves.

"And Lead Us Not into Temptation, but Deliver Us from Evil"

In the next part of the Lord's Prayer, Jesus is asking God to protect us from that which is evil and to guide us away from harm. Throughout his ministry, Jesus reminds us that there are two ways we are attacked in this world. The first way is by internal struggles, which includes temptation.

Every one of us will be tempted. A Christian therapist friend of mine says that we all have strong areas in our spiritual formation, and we all have weak areas. After Jesus' baptism, the Spirit led him into the wilderness to be tempted in all of the ways that we are tempted. (See Matthew 4:1-11; Luke 4:1-13.) The three temptations of Jesus symbolize the complete nature of how we are tempted in the world. So, yes, Jesus literally has been where we are in terms of facing Satan's arrows. But Scripture says that Jesus did not sin (Hebrews 4:15). That's what made his humanity so different from ours. Jesus knows that we are going to be tempted—it's not a matter of *if*, but *when*.

But this part of the Lord's Prayer includes two facets: *Keep us from temptation* and *deliver us from evil*. Not only does

Satan attack us with *internal* struggles and vulnerabilities; Jesus knows that we also experience *external* attacks from the evil that resides in this world. It is not enough to say, "There is evil." The real truth is that "there is evil, and it's coming for *us*." I know, it sounds like a bad horror movie. But this is a war for our morality, our attitudes, our dreams, our hope, and our possibilities. Bad things happen in this world; we know who makes them happen—and *you* are the target.

There was a big story in the national news a few years back, from Ohio, where a man had held some young women hostage in his home for many years, not far from where they had been abducted. We can talk about temptation and "troubles in our world." But that situation was just plain evil. There is no means for making sense of it apart from the abject brokenness of our world. This situation reminds us that we don't have to look much farther than our own homes, communities, and cities to see that just as we have internal attacks that are trying to distract us from our relationship with God, we also have those external situations that are simply out to destroy.

Sir George Adam Smith's great climb in the Swiss Alps displayed the power and beauty of those majestic peaks. For many years, he had wanted to climb a particular section, one that had the most jagged and difficult views. When Sir George arrived at the peak, he stood up at the edge of the cliff. The wind was more severe than many realized, including him. The native guide walking him through the passes saw Sir George about to stand. It is said that the guide grabbed him and immediately pulled him down. "Oh, no, sir," he said. "When you get to this height, you are more stable on your knees."

Jesus knew that there are some places where we are strong enough only on our knees. It's not through our own strength or knowledge that we are able to beat back the attacks of the adversary; it's only when we are positioned most humbly in front of God.

"End Where You Began"

A wise teacher friend of mine likes to say, "End where you began." With the Lord's Prayer, that would be with the concluding portion, which says, "For thine is the kingdom, and the power, and the glory, for ever" (Matthew 6:13*b* KJV). Although some codices from which this prayer was translated omit this verse, Semitic prayers always end where they start. Those prayers are cyclical in nature, in part, to keep the students focused on the most important issues for which they are praying. Thus, *if you begin with praise, you end with praise.* Except there will be one difference: Though you end where you began, the preceding prayer time affects you. You are not the same. You have bared your soul before the Creator of the universe and asked for God's intercession, forgiveness, and strength. Quite simply, your praise should mean more now.

I have used the Lord's Prayer as an outline for my prayers every day of my life since that week as a sixteen-year-old. It doesn't matter how long you've been praying or how much Bible you know; it doesn't matter how deep your devotional life has been—using the Lord's Prayer as an outline for *your* prayer changes you. Jesus knew it would. But you are not transformed by some mystical effect (though I am sure the Spirit could do that). Instead, I believe you are changed simply by giving yourself over to the process of what God will do in these moments. You will not be the same.

Remember, Jesus offered this outline from his own experience of being with the Father. This was a personal gift from Jesus. It was not an outline born from "research groups" and scholarship. This outline grew from the time the Father and Jesus spent together as Jesus would "take time away" to be with God. The Lord's Prayer is the imprint of Jesus' personal connection with the Father, shared freely with you and me.

A friend of mine teaches in a small village in Africa. This friend was teaching about beginning a new devotional and prayer life. As he would teach, the same teaching setting would unfold every week. As was normally the case, the elders would be taught first. They would gather in the center of the village, near the campfire, to listen and learn. When teaching time was finished, the elders would walk away from the village to go to their "quiet places" every morning. The elders were accustomed to "quiet places," so it was not a stretch to incorporate this idea for meditation in my friend's teaching of a devotional life.

My friend noted that as the elders walked away, they would always go in the same direction, to the same places. The weed-like grass that ran from the edge of the village into the fields was easily marked by the stamping down of the elders' paths. Therefore, the paths that were formed would remain each week. You literally could see, week after week, where the elders had left and gone to pray. Their footsteps in their spiritual journey were physically noted by these trampled paths. However, even more interesting was that some of the paths were deeper and more worn than others. Not only could you see the paths; you also could see which elder's path was most used from the faithfulness of his "time away." Eventually, as the other villagers could tell more and more of the difference between one elder's path and another's, the villagers would say to one another, "Dear brother, your path is getting awfully overgrown."

I want to ask you, is the grass overgrowing your path of prayer? Have you been there in a while? Have you seen the power of what God can do? The rest of this story—well, Jesus leaves this part up to you. He has modeled the power of prayers, of getting away with the Father, and he even shared with us an outline for how to make it all happen.

But this is where Jesus finishes. Once you give yourself over to this kind of life, a life where you are willing to pray yourself into this new relationship, where you are willing to be changed, it becomes more than just a ritual or even an outline—it becomes a lifestyle of presence in front of the Father. It's more than just showing up in front of the holy place: You're in a holy relationship, and now you are not the same.

I once learned something powerful from Acts 9. When Peter is trying to heal a girl named Tabitha, who has died, a part of this passage that I had missed all these years is when Peter gets to the point where he has to get by himself. It's just him and the girl, her body lifeless. Peter is trying to heal her, and he says, "You know what? I do not know any other power but your power, God!" And verse 40 tells us that Peter turns to the dead girl and says, "Open your eyes, for it's time for you to get up!" (paraphrased).

Jesus is looking at your life right now, your marriage, your finances, your service, and he is saying, "Open your eyes; it's time for you to get up. It's time for you to take hold of a prayer life that will change you." God does not want to just walk by you; he wants to be living inside every aspect of who you are.

There's a phrase in business known as "eating your own dog

food." I didn't know of this concept until I heard about it from some friends of mine. Apparently "eating your own dog food" means that when you are trying to sell something, you first demonstrate that you use it in your own life. There's a story about J. P. Morgan, the great banker, who was trying to turn people on to the idea of using electric lightbulbs. People were scared to death of Thomas Edison's new invention—they thought electricity would cause their homes to go up in flames. So Morgan did the only thing he could: He put electric lights in his own house first. Morgan had Edison put a generator in the basement, and he had four hundred lightbulbs installed inside his Manhattan home. Edison flipped the switch, and light was everywhere. People were amazed and awed, and guess what? From that moment on, everybody wanted electric lights in their houses.

Are you trying to sell a gospel that you don't really believe, that doesn't show up first in your own life? Are you talking about the power and the love and the grace and the forgiveness of a God that you yourself have not been able to shine in the very darkest places of your own life? The best place that our witness begins is right here. I love what Bill Hybels says in his book *Too Busy Not to Pray*: "If the request [you make of God] is wrong, God says, 'No.' If the timing is wrong, God says, 'Slow.' If you are wrong, God says, 'Grow.' But if the request is right, the timing is right and your heart is right, God says, 'Go!'"[3]

Are you ready to go? to do more than just say the words? Are you ready to become the very heart of prayer, focusing on the heart of God, ushering in forgiveness, bringing about a new relationship, standing against evil and temptation, becoming the very power and presence of a God who not only changes your life, but also changes the world?

Our Father who art in heaven, hallowed be thy name. Thy kingdom come, thy will be done on earth as it is in heaven. Give us this day our daily bread, and forgive us our trespasses, as we forgive those who trespass against us. And lead us not into temptation, but deliver us from evil. For thine is the kingdom and the power and the glory for ever and ever. Amen.[4]

*T*hen Jesus went with his disciples to a place called Gethsemane.

Then he went a short distance farther and fell on his face and prayed, "My Father, if it's possible, take this cup of suffering away from me. However—not what I want but what you want."

He came back to the disciples and found them sleeping. He said to Peter, "Couldn't you stay alert one hour with me? Stay alert and pray so that you won't give in to temptation. The spirit is eager, but the flesh is weak."

A second time he went away and prayed, "My Father, if it's not possible that this cup be taken away unless I drink it, then let it be what you want."

Again he came and found them sleeping. Their eyes were heavy with sleep. But he left them and again went and prayed the same words for the third time.

Matthew 26:36, 39-44

Conclusion

"WE ARE HOW WE PRAY"

Jesus wants us to do more than spend thirty minutes in a good devotional time (which is important). He wants our prayers to become the blueprint for the person we claim to be and for the person others claim they see when we are around.

My Friend John and His Grandmother's Words

My friend John is a praying man. In fact, all of his life, prayer has resonated as more than words; it's been the doorway to his relationship with God. He told of learning to pray from his grandmother, a wonderful, mighty saint who "prayed like her life depended on it." But her prayers did not stop simply as words hanging in the air. She always told John, "Our prayers mean little if we aren't courageous enough to live them." John never forgot those words.

He left his small, northern Arkansas hometown not long after high school; attended the University of Tennessee; and then earned a law degree from Yale University. As John described himself, he was "a good churchgoing boy," and he always remembered to say his prayers, just as his grandmother had taught him. His journey took him first to Atlanta and then to Memphis. His life was filled with success, family, and all the accomplishments a smart Southern boy could imagine.

When John retired from practicing law, he settled into his Memphis home, and he volunteered at local ministry shelters and at his church. He took over the day-to-day operations of the old family business, and he enjoyed the life he had worked so hard to establish. All the while, he prayed daily and, as he liked to say, "tried to live as faithful to life as life had been to me." From most accounts, it was a journey well lived.

But John felt as though something was missing. Sure, he had tried to live a good life and remain faithful to all the lessons those who loved him had taught him from a young age. Yet, as he grew older, he felt as though God wanted something more from him.

John enrolled in a prayer ministry class at his local church, and he began praying the Lord's Prayer from a much different angle and with a different focus than he had at any time before in his life. The prayer class taught him to pause and truly soak in what it meant to be in the presence of the Creator of the universe; it taught him what *daily bread* meant—for those who had it and for those who didn't—and what it truly meant to be delivered from the evil of this world. The result was a conversation started deep inside of John's soul that would not cease.

He talked with his pastor and several trusted friends about the stirrings in his soul. Each of them offered great advice, but John knew the real answers were not so much in a plan or a process as in the personal ways God wanted to meet John through his prayers. John began spending more focused time with God, not so much praying or talking as listening. He was amazed at what you can hear God say to your soul when you stop long enough to really take it all in. The words were fresh, powerful, and, at times, critical of places where John had missed opportunities to be the hands and feet of Jesus.

These prayer moments with God became journaling and study opportunities, eventually leading to various other ways in which John sought God's guidance and wisdom throughout the days and weeks. The more John spent time with God, the more his decisions, thoughts, values, and impressions of the world around him changed. He stopped seeing the world through the veil of his own wants and desires, and he actually began to see the world through the eyes of Christ. Most of what he saw engaged him and brought him a sense of inner wholeness. But other parts of what he saw in a world broken apart from God's original intentions tore at John's heart. The closer he drew to God, the more he saw what God saw, and it troubled him.

One area where John saw the world differently was in hunger and poverty among the most vulnerable people on the planet. In particular, John became concerned with the needs of orphans starving in sub-Saharan Africa. As difficult as the circumstances were in many areas, equally disturbing was the simplicity with which these issues could be addressed but weren't. The reasons were many and played from the all-too-familiar song sheet of corruption, cultural distinctions, and prejudice. But the answers remained fairly attainable, though the questions themselves caused many, at times, to be uncomfortable.

John was a fan of Dr. Norman Borlaug, the man who had invented a first version of dwarf wheat. This strain of wheat could grow and develop but would not fall over and become susceptible to insects and drought. In fact, Dr. Borlaug was credited with saving more than one billion lives with this discovery.[1] John loved the simple description of one stalk of wheat, previously unusable in so many parts of the world, now available for mass distribution to those in need. But before John knew what he was supposed to do with the rumblings in his spirit, Norman Borlaug passed away.

While attending the memorial service for Dr. Borlaug, John met a group of people who specialized in providing usable bags of wheat and other food sources to starving areas of the world. Unlike other distribution methods, these one-family bags needed only water, and a family instantly would have a porridge-like substance that provided the nutrients people needed to survive. John prayed about how God could use him to distribute these bags of wheat.

Arriving back at his church, John set up the first of several packing days whereby volunteers could help fill the family food bags, label them for distribution, and then pack them in crates to send to the hardest-hit areas of the world. Not knowing how many people would attend the first of these packing days, John prepared to put together, at most, thirty thousand bags of wheat—a noble gesture for a first-time ministry.

By the end of the first week, more than four hundred thousand bags of wheat had been prepared for shipping. And as the first season of packing days finished, nearly two million bags had been constructed. What began as the simple prayers of a man looking for God's next steps became a regimen of hope that would change and save lives halfway around the world.

Today, John's small ministry venture has grown into a successful mission project that not only feeds hungry people in countries around the world; it also offers spiritual nourishment for the families across the street who are working to put the bags together for hungry souls around the world. How did this happen? One could say it was the ingenuity of brilliant men and women following the example of another brilliant man.

And yes, it is true that the cause of grace and hope often unfold one life, one introduction, and one intersection at a time.

But before all of that, as important as those moments were, I believe the help millions of people received through John's efforts and leadership started at the knee of his grandmother, as she was reminding him that his prayers matter. My friend John, with all that he became in this world, is first and foremost how he prayed.

The Pretty Little Girl in the Portrait

My first church as a pastor was very small. We had around forty-five people who worshiped with us regularly. The vast majority of them (about 95 percent) were over the age of sixty-five. In fact, we joked that if you were under sixty, you were in the youth group. They were an incredible group of saints who loved the Lord, served faithfully, and prayed diligently.

One particular woman, whom I will call Pat, invited my wife and me to her house on a regular basis. She was a wonderful cook, and she loved having the preacher over for lunch, dinner, or dessert.

On one visit to Pat's home, I discovered a beautiful painting of a little girl kneeling and praying in a field of daisies. The little girl had her hands clasped and her eyes closed and wore the sweetest smile. As I looked closely at the picture, I noticed that there was a gentle tear coming down the edge of her cheek. It was subtle, and not clearly visible except by the person who took time to study it.

I stood there looking at the painting, wondering what was going on in that little girl's life. With such a sweet smile in such a wonderful setting, what would cause her to cry? Were they tears of joy? Was there something we could not see? What could it be?

I walked back into the dining room, where my hostess was preparing another of her delicious dishes to serve. "You were looking at the painting," she said.

"Yes," I answered. "It is just so beautiful." She could tell that I was considering something I had seen.

"You want to know about the tear?" Pat asked. I was surprised at her insight, yet I knew that anyone who had spent enough time with the painting would be interested in this small-but-powerful detail.

"Yes," I said. "It seems so subtle, and yet it screams at you the longer you look at it."

"The little girl in the painting came from a broken family," my friend answered. "She was the apple of her father's eye until he found another family to love more. He left the girl, her mother, and her sisters and moved a thousand miles away."

"What happened to her? Was that why she was crying?" I asked.

"Sort of," my friend said. "After her mother and father divorced, she would go into the field next to her house. It was full of daisies. She liked to kneel and pray. She talked to God frequently. When her father left her, she found a new Father to take his place."

"And the tear?" I asked.

"The tear was when she realized that this Father would never leave. He would never abandon her."

"How do you know all of this?" I inquired.

"Well," my friend said softly, "I'm that little girl."

I had not known her story. She went on to tell me of how her father had made attempts to reconnect with her, but how eventually he would let her down one time after another. He was a good man, just not a good father. By the end of his life, he lived in the shadow of much regret and, most important, without his daughter.

Through it all, my friend learned to pray. She didn't pray because it was the right thing to do or because it was part of her daily devotional. No, she prayed in the field of daisies and late at night and in the deepest, most personal places because it was where she met the One who would never let her down. Her prayers became a testament to what real relationship in faith could be. Her prayers became the language of her life.

Father, I want those you gave me to be with me where I am. Then they can see my glory, which you gave me because you loved me before the creation of the world.

Righteous Father, even the world didn't know you, but I've known you, and these believers know that you sent me. I've made your name known to them and will continue to make it known so that your love for me will be in them, and I myself will be in them.

John 17:24-26

My friend Pat was a wonderful person of faith. She loved the Lord. And she knew the difference between simply saying she loved God and actually clinging to him for survival. For every daisy she picked and prayed over, God embraced her little heart, dried her tears, and painted a picture that never grew old. *She* grew older, and her life took many twists and turns. Yet in so many ways, she was still that little girl kneeling in the field. No matter how many years passed, like all of us, *she was how she prayed*.

Confronting the Bad Things with the Better Things

We live in a world where bad things happen. And we live in a world where people do bad things. But Jesus' prayers push toward the belief that we don't have to be overwhelmed by those two truths. Yes, we face a host of sins that define and distract us. We are tempted, and we confront evil time and again. But the Lord's Prayer clearly says that the God of the universe believes enough in you and me to stand in the gap of those temptations and to protect us from that evil.

That part of the prayer reminds me that God confronts the bad things in our lives with better things. What are those things? Simply, spending time with God and then living in the world as though you have spent time with the Creator. It really is that straightforward. Most of us underestimate the importance of proximity when it comes to fighting the weakest parts of our spiritual constitutions. But nothing substitutes for being in the presence of God.

When my middle daughter was five years old, another kid bullied her in her class. We did not know the full extent of the problem until we went to a Sunday-school class party and the little girl's family was there. We noticed that our daughter, who is always the life of the party, stayed very close to us. When we asked her about it later, she replied that the little girl had been picking on her. Where did our daughter run? She ran to her parents. We were her safe place.

The same is true for our relationship with God. Sometimes the world bullies us. It often pushes us around. The adversary wants nothing more than to destroy us. When it all gets to be too much, we draw close to God. We run to the Father. God is our safe place.

What if we didn't have to be in that place? What if we could face our nightmares and struggles long before they haunt us and taunt us? That is Jesus' prayer. The God who is God of heaven and earth, who is strong and certain, who is standing at the center of our needs—that God will stand around the corner for us too, waiting in the shadows well ahead of where we have to go. Run to him. You don't have to be afraid.

My Grandfather's Saying: "I Am How I Pray"

As I mentioned earlier in this book, for years, my grandfather used a phrase when describing parts of his spiritual journey. He would say, "I am how I pray." I loved the phrase from the moment I first heard it, although I really didn't appreciate its meaning until much later.

Over the course of my ministry, I have seen many examples of people who "lived as they prayed"—both from the positive and negative side. And just as my grandfather insisted, the condition of their prayer lives dictated so much of what would become of their journey.

Of course, I am chief among the suspects in this conversation. As one who has faced so many struggles in my life—hemophilia, becoming HIV-positive from medical treatment for my hemophilia, contracting hepatitis C from meds for treatment, open heart surgery, diabetes, high blood pressure, liver damage, and so on—I have been conscious of my every thought, decision, and intention. And there is no better marker for the next steps of my life than how and what my prayer life points to in me.

Like everyone else, my journey looks like that of one who "is as he prays." And to describe or measure the ups and downs of my life, one only has to look at my prayer journal for an accurate time line or map of the outcomes.

That is why I am so thankful for what I have learned in the course of writing this book. To know that Jesus not only agreed with my grandfather's statement but basically lived his own life as a model or example of the truth is humbling. I have mentioned to several friends that there are countless books on prayer and the praying life, but that there are very few on the prayer life of Jesus. I hope that will change now.

As I shared the moments of when Jesus slipped away to be alone with the Father, or when he prayed in the midst of difficult situations, or when he simply found prayer as his only solace or choice for approaching the earthly pain and sorrow his humanity encountered, I felt closer to him than ever before. Sure, I still call him Lord and Savior; I am in awe of his power and presence. But I have to admit, there are moments when I can see him sitting under the tree, on the side of the hill, or around the campfire, and I can almost hear him beckon me to sit with him. And so I limp my ailing body and soul over to where he is, and I feel well and whole, even if only for a moment.

The prayers of Jesus are more than words. They are about the quiet places that caused even the Son of God to pause and breathe in the presence of the Father. They are also loud, victorious places where Jesus says, "Yes, I knew they would get it!" And finally, the prayers of Jesus are about a Son who had given everything for this mission of grace and reconciliation for God's people. It had to be lonely and so different for Jesus, who, as Philippians 2 reminds us, had known a different existence before this. But there, along the dusty roads and next to the lapping waters of the Sea of Galilee, we find Jesus taking the steps that we just could not take for ourselves. With all the stories that give me glimpses of Jesus' life and humanity, nothing is more powerful to me than to know that while he made the journey, he also took time away to stay in touch with his Father. And maybe even sweeter in the whole scene is to know that they actually spent much of their time talking about you and me. As my teenage children would say, "How crazy cool and undeniably humbling is that?"

Considering how often we Christians miss the boat for one another throughout our journey in this world, this may be the most important example Jesus teaches: that in spite of all of us who respond to each other, "I will be praying for you," and then rarely keep our promise, the God of the universe rarely said it, but on frequent days and early mornings, "slipped away" to do just that. With all that we so quickly want to criticize God for regarding how the world "is," probably the best reason to take note of him is that as the fog of doubt clears and uncertainties reemerge, the one person you can most count on to see next *is* *God.* Prayer does that. And I, for one, am deeply thankful.

A Final Word of Challenge and Thanks

With all of my books, the final words are the most difficult for me to write. So many people play a part in making each and every project special, and this latest effort has been no exception. Once again, the congregation I have the privilege of leading (Christ UMC in Memphis) has played a tremendous role in encouraging and supporting my writing and teaching ministry. I literally could not do this part of my God-given calling without them. And, of course, I would not be the person I am without the love and care of my dear, sweet family. Pokey, Sarai Grace, Juli Anna, and Emma Leigh are my reasons for jumping (or at least slowly sliding) out of bed each morning. I am pumped at the potential that God has for each of my girls, and it is a joy to watch God's hand in their lives.

I also am thankful for a set of friends, supporters, and staff who walk so faithfully with me through both good and not-so-good times. What would I do without Scott Lees, Karen Goff, Bob Whitsitt, Anthony Thaxton, Bo Parker, Emily Matheny,

and Tom Fuerst—along with countless others—who participate with me on what I believe is the best church staff in the
country? We are a family, and that means so much to me at
this place and season of my life. Of course, two of those "family members" stand out: Maxie Dunnam is more than just my
mentor and colleague; he has become the dearest of friends.
And my assistant, Anita Jones, is the rock and lighthouse for
stabilizing and setting the course of my crazy schedule, life, and
responsibilities. Their support, prayers, and encouragement
mean more than I have words to express.

There are also so many friends who stand in the gap with
me, not just in these projects, but in every step of my life—Jack
Moore, Doug McKnight, Bill Rhodes, Michael Drake, Bob
Buckman, Mike Weaver, Bryan Jordan, Brad Martin, Scott
Morris, and so many others at Christ Church and beyond.

Finally, but certainly not last, there have been those who
have prayed for me from the beginning, from my first steps to
my latest book, and without them, I am not the person I am
today. Mom, Buford, Whitney, Nanny, Patty, and Dad, once
again, one more prayer—keep them coming!

For this book, I have felt such a sense of urgency. Not just
because of the circumstances of my life, with my health struggles and questions, but for the Church in general. As I wrote
this book, I couldn't help but hear Christ's prayerful words in

the daily struggles I see around me. As Jesus prayed for unity, it was almost as though he looked across time and space to speak those very words for where the body of Christ is today.

Today, more than ever, the Church needs those who will stand on the mountain and proclaim the beauty of the Good News that still changes lives. It needs those who will implore us to live lives that bring glory to God; those who will offer penance for when we trust the world's wisdom and not our Holy God's; and those who will then beg for mercy as we pray for unity once more.

I pray you will be one who will answer that call. And I pray too that you and others who will read this book will fall on your knees. We are stronger in that position.

Praise God.

Appendix

THE PRAYERS OF JESUS IN SCRIPTURE

Following are some basic questions and answers about the prayer life of Jesus, as well as scriptural references and notations (in chronological order for the writing of the books listed) to the prayers of Jesus used in the development of this book. This is not an exhaustive list of the prayers of Jesus, nor is the book focused only on the specific moments of when the Gospels described Jesus praying. As Oswald Chambers insisted, most of our spiritual journey is the "way of a Sacrament out here." The "out here" are the normal, ordinary ways that our spiritual connection to God informs our walk, interaction, hopes, dreams, fears, and so on. Through his Incarnation, Jesus experienced the fullness of humanity, meaning that he understands our potential and problems firsthand. Jesus' earthly ministry, including all of the disciplines he himself clearly practiced, provide for the incredible presence of God through all the elements of an ordinary life. Again referring to Oswald Chambers, the spiritual interaction between God the Father and God the Son is an "open house for the universe" by which we are offered a special invitation.

Therefore, this book takes the more than five dozen references of Jesus' prayers and frames not only the focus of Jesus' prayer life in the moment of their being prayed but the residual effect of what such "holy communication" means for all of us. Thus, to understand the true intimacy and power of the prayers of Jesus is to comprehend how Jesus' prayer life affected his earthly walk and ours.

Included are instances when Jesus prayed publicly and also occasions when he "went away" to be alone with the Father. There are also references to where Jesus instructed the disciples and the community of followers in how to pray and the impact of prayer upon their lives. However, there are also several examples of how prayer framed the purpose of Jesus' ministry with the disciples long after the actual prayer had been prayed. Before Paul ever suggested that we pray "without ceasing" (1 Thessalonians 5:17 KJV), Jesus modeled it. And, the lack of prayer as an effective tool of the disciples remains a constant theme running throughout Jesus' ministry with the disciples. For example, in Jesus and the disciples' encounter with the man who brought his son to be healed (Mark 9), though the Gospel records Jesus as praying only once, several chapters surround, first, Jesus' specific prayer for the disciples to witness the glory of the Father, but second, the continued "need" for growth and depth in the disciples' prayer life for such difficult interactions as with the father and the demon-possessed son. Thus, it is natural and, I believe, important to assume that Jesus was consistently praying during this period for this "awakening" in his disciple's lives.

The scriptural notations as well as the "ongoing conversation" work together to form a complete picture of Jesus' prayer life and the importance of prayer in his ministry, his daily routine, and the development of those who followed him. Closing out my honoring of Oswald Chambers, you see, through the prayer life of Jesus, a continued "casting of bread upon the water."

Take some time to look through the passages and familiarize yourself with them. The more you know about them, the more you will understand why these passages cast such a large shadow upon Jesus' ministry journey during his time on earth. But, also remember, like any of us, the power and importance of prayer did not stop at "amen" for Jesus.

How many prayer moments of Jesus are recorded in the four Gospels and the Book of Acts?

There are more than sixty times in the Gospels and the Book of Acts when Jesus prays or takes time away to meditate. These prayers of Jesus fit into different models or methods, including times Jesus went away to pray, times he prayed in public, occasions when he engaged in meditation and what modern readers would call "devotions," times he prayed about a person or a situation, times he prayed with the disciples about an issue, and times when the "ongoing conversation" of prayer sits at the center of Jesus' interactions with the disciples and others.

However, though the prayers of Jesus are varied, regardless of the method or setting, they fit into one of these five categories, and they represent a certain pattern that Jesus modeled regarding his own values and the implementation of prayer in his earthly life. Prayer was an important part of Jesus' ministry, and one has the sense that prayer as a practice of his relationship with God the Father started early and went deep in Jesus' walk on this earth.

What was Jesus' basic routine for his prayer life?

As mentioned previously, Jesus had various methods he followed in his prayer life. Jesus liked to go away and spend time with the Father in private moments of prayerful conversation. He also liked using prayer in groups with his disciples and other followers, particularly to bless and to sanctify the presence of God's Spirit and work within a situation. Jesus also prayed, as we do, in times of great personal and corporate need, spending time addressing not only the needs of the faithful, but also his own circumstances as well. And Jesus prayed for guidance and intercession for the people he met in his journey. One notion of Jesus' prayer life and routine was the inclusion of prayer as a personal experience or conversation with the Father. This was deepened by Jesus' earthly needs and encounters. And yet, he fully expected his disciples to include this same level of prayer in their own lives and ministries.

What was the prayer life routine typically like for a Jewish rabbi (teacher)?

Jesus' Jewish heritage greatly influenced his life from start to finish, and he had great respect for the customs and rituals expected of a teacher in his culture. Like any faithful Jew, Jesus paid his Temple taxes (Matthew 17:24-27), attended synagogue (Matthew 5:23, 24), and observed the festivals and holidays of the Jewish calendar. And for each of the ways in which he celebrated his Jewish faith, Jesus carefully used the connection of his heritage as a teaching tool for his followers. For instance, he used the traditional prayers that any rabbi would use for occasions such as meals, rest, and the morning.

Also, the Gospels indicate that Jesus was quite Jewish in his dress and his mannerisms. For instance, we are told that when the woman with the bleeding condition reached for him, she "touched the hem of his clothes" (Matthew 9:20; Luke 8:44; see also Mark 6:56). The Greek term used here, *kraspedon*, commonly translates the Hebrew as *tzitzit* or "fringes," which God had commanded the Jewish people to wear (Numbers 15:37-41).

Jesus' way of life reflected other Jewish customs as well, including the use of open-air preaching (as was a custom of the contemporary rabbis of Jesus' day) and the use of baptism to welcome new followers. Jesus practiced his Jewishness completely and to the end of his earthly ministry. Jesus was orthodox in his respect and response to the Law. He declared the permanence of the whole Torah (Matthew 5:17-19) and even accepted Pharisaic extensions (Matthew 23:2-3). Therefore, Jesus was firmly rooted in his heritage as a Jewish teacher and remained faithful to the customs and teachings so he would not be disqualified. But Jesus also expanded the use of the Jewish customs to offer a new way of understanding prayer, the Law, and the varied customs of his heritage.

How was prayer viewed by the religious leaders of Jesus' day?

As noted previously, prayer was part of a set of religious obligations that the religious leaders believed were critical to sharing faith and practice with God and God's people. But this practice was within the nature and setting of the community of the faithful for the most part, and it did not express a personal relationship or conversation between the divine and humanity. Therefore, there was a special connection between God and God's people in prayer, but not as that which would be modeled by Jesus' relationship with the Father. Jesus opens the door (and a few windows too) by making prayer personal and part of the daily routine with God.

How does the prayer life of Jesus relate to our understanding and practice of prayer today?

The prayer life of Jesus is the primary model for our modern understanding and practice of prayer as both an experience between humanity and God, and for humanity to relate itself, its desires, and its needs to God's will. The prayer life of Jesus also connects the general experience of the community of the faithful to God's heart, providing for the first time in creation a true conversation for the Creator and humanity. This shift cannot be overstated, particularly in light of what the coming of the Holy Spirit after Jesus would mean for all of us. There was no need for intermediaries, training, special considerations or places, or qualifications in order to talk with God. Instead, Jesus provided an open communication system between the Creator and creation.

Jesus Praying and Teaching on Prayer in the Gospel of Mark

Mark 1:35—Jesus goes away to pray and be with the Father.

Mark 6:46—Jesus sends the disciples away to pray and then

goes up on the mountainside to pray. This is just after Jesus fed the five thousand and the disciples did not understand.

Mark 9:7—This is at the Transfiguration, and God has just spoken back to Jesus. This is not the usual "more than words," but it symbolizes the deep connection between God the Father and Jesus, and how Jesus' regular time with the Father manifests itself in such big moments as this.

Mark 9:29—Here the disciples ask Jesus why they themselves could not cast out the demon from the boy. Jesus says it has a direct correlation with prayer and the prayer life. I like this because it ties back to Jesus' own prayer life, since he suggests that it was the reason why, in his humanity, he needed a strong prayer life as well.

Mark 11:24—Jesus instructs the disciples about the power of prayer and how one can move a mountain through it. This is in response to a very troubling section where Jesus is hungry, curses the fig tree, and then turns over the tables in the Temple.

Mark 14:32-42—Jesus prays for peace in the garden of Gethsemane. This is probably the most important of all the prayer moments for Jesus' ministry.

Mark 15:34—Jesus lets out a loud cry upon the cross: "My God, my God, why have you left me?"

Jesus Praying and Teaching on Prayer in the Gospel of Matthew

Matthew 5:44—Jesus says to pray for those who harass you, indicating that he prays that prayer as well.

Matthew 6:5-6—Jesus gives us a glimpse into how he prays in private.

Matthew 6:7-15—This is the passage about the Lord's Prayer and Jesus' instructions to pray as he directs. It is an outline covering the major issues of what prayer is supposed to be, in Jesus' eyes.

Matthew 11:25-26—Jesus talks to the Father as he is describing the future of Capernaum and Bethsaida. After this, Jesus tells those who are struggling hard and carrying heavy loads to come to him.

Matthew 14:13-14—Jesus learns of the death of John the Baptist and goes away to a lonely place, most likely to pray.

Matthew 14:19—Jesus prays to the Father to multiply the fishes and loaves.

Matthew 14:23—When they have fed the masses, Jesus sends the disciples ahead in a boat and goes away to pray. He then walks on the water to them.

Matthew 15:36—Jesus once again blesses and thanks God for the fishes and loaves, used this time to feed a crowd of four thousand.

Matthew 18:19-20—Jesus talks about the power of prayer, but in community relationship: the more who agree, the more power is released.

Matthew 19:13-15—Children are brought to Jesus for him to lay hands upon them and pray for them. The disciples think he is wasting time, but Jesus says this is very important.

Matthew 21:13—Jesus is angry because the merchants have turned the Temple into a house of thieves instead of a house of prayer. Prayer is the central concept for why the Temple exists.

Matthew 26:36-44—Jesus makes his way to the garden of Gethsemane. This is an important scene illustrating the power of prayer and its personal nature to Jesus. He encourages the disciples to stay alert and pray because it is the only way to be safe from temptation. In the garden, Jesus prays three different times: (1) for peace; (2) for clarity; and (3) for release.

Matthew 27:46—Jesus cries out upon the cross: "My God, my God, why have you left me?"

Jesus Praying and Teaching on Prayer in the Gospel of Luke

Luke 4:42—Jesus retreats to a deserted place after he confronts the people at the synagogue in Nazareth.

Luke 5:16—As the news of Jesus spreads, more and more people want to be near him, but he retreats at times to deserted places to pray.

Luke 6:12—Jesus prays all night long before he chooses his apostles.

Luke 6:28—Jesus tells the disciples, "Pray for those who mistreat you."

Luke 9:18—After feeding the crowds, Jesus goes to pray by himself. The disciples find him, and he asks them, "Who do the crowds say that I am?"

Luke 9:28-35—Jesus takes the three apostles with him to the mountain to pray; the Transfiguration happens during this prayer time.

Luke 10:21-22—Jesus prays a prayer of rejoicing after the return of the seventy-two.

Luke 11:1-4—Jesus teaches the disciples to pray; this is a copy from the Matthew 6 passage of the Lord's Prayer.

Luke 22:39—Jesus retreats to the Mount of Olives, "as was his custom."

Luke 22:41-46—This is the story of Jesus praying in Gethsemane.

Luke 23:34—Jesus prays, "Father, forgive them, for they don't know what they're doing."

Luke 23:46—Jesus prays, "Father, into your hands I entrust my life."

Jesus Praying and Teaching on Prayer in the Gospel of John

John 6:11-12—Jesus "gives thanks" for the bread and fish that he uses to feed the multitudes.

John 8:28-29—Jesus mentions his daily connection with the Father as the source of his authority and his message to the disciples.

John 11:41-42—Jesus speaks directly to the Father at the tomb of Lazarus. Lazarus is raised from the tomb.

John 14:16-17—Jesus promises that he will ask the Father to send the Holy Spirit to live inside those who follow Jesus. This passage sets the context for all of chapter 14.

John 15:9-15—Jesus discusses how his conversations with the Father set the stage for how we should love one another.

John 16:23-24—Jesus discusses the process of asking the

Father for what the disciples need, in his name. It is a first attempt to promote prayer as the form of communication with God.

John 17—This entire chapter is a prayer from Jesus to the Father. Jesus prays for the disciples, for unity, and for clarity; this is the key chapter that sets the framework of Jesus' prayer life.

The Disciples' Prayer in the Book of Acts

Acts 1:24-26—This is the first prayer of the disciples after Jesus' resurrection. It is a sharp departure from their earlier attitude. Before anything else happens, as Jesus has just left them, they pray. I included this Scripture reference to show how prayer had become both important and personal for the disciples. As mentioned earlier, the notion of a "way of Sacrament out here" informed both the disciples' presents and futures in following Jesus. We know that from this moment, as each would give his life for his belief in Christ, the disciples "got" it, practiced it, and, eventually, shared it with the world.

NOTES

Prayer Focus 1: Jesus Prays for Our Relationship with the Father

1. "LifeWay Research Finds Reason Adults Switch Churches," accessed May 4, 2015, www.lifeway.com/Article/LifeWay-Research -finds-reason-adults-switch-churches.
2. Dănuţ Mănăstireanu, "Perichoresis and the Early Christian Doctrine of God," *Archævs: Studies in History of Religions* 11–12 (2007–2008): 61–93, www.academia.edu/4794642/Perichore sis_and_the_Early_Christian_Doctrine_of_God.
3. Clayton Pepper, "Friendship Evangelism: The Kind Everybody Can Practice," *Church Growth Magazine*, October–December 1994, 9–10, 12.

Prayer Focus 2: Jesus Prays for God's Wisdom and Guidance in Us

1. Pamela Rose Williams, "Martin Luther Quotes: 21 Powerful Sayings," accessed May 5, 2015, www.whatchristianswanttoknow .com/martin-luther-quotes-21-powerful-sayings/.

Prayer Focus 3: Jesus Prays for Our Unity

1. Mike Preston, "Working together brings us new hope," Essex

Chronicle (UK), November 4, 2010, www.essexchronicle.co.uk
/Working-brings-new-hope/story-12624470-detail/story.html

2. Tavis Smiley, *Death of a King: The Real Story of Dr. Martin Luther King Jr.'s Final Year* (New York: Little, Brown, 2014), 236–37.

3. Ibid., 242.

4. John Wesley, "Thoughts upon Methodism," August 4, 1786.

Prayer Focus 4: Jesus Prays for Lives that Bring Glory to God

1. Leonard Sweet, *11 Indispensable Relationships You Can't Be Without* (Colorado Springs: David C. Cook, 2012), 20.

2. J. Kirk Johnson, *Why Christians Sin: Avoiding the Dangers of an Uncommitted Life* (Grand Rapids: Discovery House, 1992), 142.

3. John Wesley, "The Methodist Covenant Prayer," on the website of the Methodist Church in Great Britain, accessed March 6, 2015, www.methodist.org.uk/who-we-are/what-is-distinctive-about -methodism/a-covenant-with-god.

Prayer Focus 5: Jesus Prays for Our Consistency in Prayer

1. William Nicholson, *Shadowlands* (New York: Samuel French, 1989), 81.

2. Dietrich Bonhoeffer, *The Cost of Discipleship* (New York: Touchstone, 1995), 185.

3. Bill Hybels, *Too Busy Not to Pray: Slowing Down to Be with God,* rev. and exp. (Downers Grove, IL: InterVarsity Press, 2008), 86.

4. The Book of Common Prayer (1928), http://justus.anglican.org /resources/bcp/1928/Family_Prayer.htm.

Conclusion: "We Are How We Pray"

1. David Macaray, "The Man Who Saved a Billion Lives," October 15, 2013, *Huffington Post: World*, www.huffingtonpost.com/david-macaray/the-man-who-saved-a-billi_b_4099523.html.

Study Guide Available for Group Use

Study the purpose of Jesus' prayers with your Bible study group or Sunday school class.

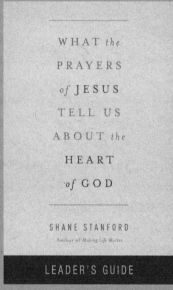

WHAT *the*
PRAYERS
of JESUS
TELL US
ABOUT *the*
HEART
of GOD

SHANE STANFORD
Author of *Making Life Matter*

LEADER'S GUIDE

- Five sessions coordinate with each of the five chapters of the book.
- Discussion questions engage group interaction.
- Group activities and easy-to-reproduce handouts provided for life application.
- Additional leader prompts, summaries, and insights included.